The Day His Heart Stopped Crying

A Sinner's Journey to Grace Through
Heartbreak and Sorrow

Angela Kennecke

Angela Kennecke

* * *

Disclaimer: *Through interviews with the author, the author has tried to recreate events, locales and conversations from Steve Frey's memories of them. This is Steve Frey's recollection of events and he has related them to the author to the best of his knowledge. In order to maintain their anonymity in some instances, the author has changed the names of individuals and places.*

* * *

ISBN: 1545572976
ISBN-13: 978-1545572979

DEDICATION

Zachariah John, Jeremiah Glen, Hannah Marie, and Dinah Joan: I love and deeply respect you, my children. Please forgive me, for all my shortcomings. Your love for me is the greatest gift any father could receive!

Steven Frey

God Bless you as
you read this book!

Geoffrey

Prologue: A Judas Among Us

"For if they fall, one will lift up his fellow. But woe to him who is alone when he falls and has not another to lift him up!"
Ecclesiastes 4:10

A rambunctious group of high school boys crowded into the small café on Main Street called *Little Brick Ice Cream*. The homemade ice cream was the creation of Marie Frey. Her husband, Steve, broasted the chicken and served it with gusto. Football players, ranging in age from 15 to 18, were starving after their rigorous drills. The coach had been especially hard on them this warm September afternoon. They had just finished their daily practice, and it was tradition for them to head down to *Little Brick* afterwards on Wednesdays to get all the broasted chicken, potato wedges, nachos and ice cream they could eat for just $5. It was a high school boy's favorite kind of meal: hot, greasy, fattening and filling. But they also enjoyed spending time riddling "Frey," as they called the proprietor of the place.

At 65, Frey was an old man to these young boys. He had a full head of thick, salt-and-pepper hair and a steel gray mustache. Frey *always* wore blue denim overalls. He typically sported his silver-rimmed spectacles. Behind them were large blue eyes, known to occasionally tear up when the boys told him how much they cared about him — not outright, so much, but rather in the form of a "See, ya' later, Mr. Frey!" Or, "Your chicken is the best in town, Mr. Frey!" Or simply by the fact that they came back every Wednesday evening.

The truth was, at first, the boys just thought Frey was an odd, little old man, maybe even a little crazy. But as time went on and their Wednesday visits sometimes turned into two or more visits a week, the boys realized that Frey's love for them was real. It was the unique combination of the love of a father or grandfather and a friend. And it was a love they were going to rely on during the weeks to come. You see, that Wednesday night in the middle of September when the Platte-Geddes, South Dakota football team gathered inside the *Little Brick,* would be the last time they would all be together.

None of them saw it coming; not a single one could have imagined the horror that would rock this tiny town of 1,244 people. Nothing like it had ever happened here before, and nothing of this magnitude was likely to ever happen again. Platte is a mostly agricultural town, just a few miles east of Platte Creek, a tributary of the Missouri River, that cuts the rural, wind-blown state of South Dakota in half. Just a few miles to the south and east of Platte is the border of the Yankton Sioux Reservation. But Platte itself is about 95 percent white. All the boys on the team were typical, Midwestern teenagers; nothing very interesting had happened in their young lives to this point. But their innocence and trust in their community was about to be shattered.

Michael Westerhuis, a 16-year-old boy who clearly benefitted from his German heritage in strength on the field and self-discipline, was part of the group of boys who filled the *Little Brick* that sweet September night. Michael had poked his wavy, blonde head back inside the café, after he left with a group of boys. Upon realizing that one of his teammates didn't have a ride, he had returned to offer him one.

It was Michael's last selfless act. At 5:35 the next morning, a 9-1-1 call came in. A transient working in the area and staying at the local campground called to report a fire that looked like it had been burning for some time. The shrill sounds of the fire whistle in the center of town awakened everyone on Thursday, Sept. 17, 2015. Members of the Platte Volunteer Fire Department hopped out of their beds and were soon rushing to the scene. It was the Westerhuis place two miles south of Platte, and the fire was raging out of control. Firefighters from neighboring towns arrived a short time later, and it took all their resources and efforts to knock the fire down. Once it was safe to go inside the still-smoldering building, the firefighters made a grim discovery — all six members of the Westerhuis family had died. Nine-year-old Kailey, 10-year-old Jaeci, 14-year-old Connor and 16-year-old Michael all perished, along with their mother, Nicole, and their father, Scott.

Days later, the community would learn from investigators that the unthinkable had happened: Scott Westerhuis had shot and killed his entire family before setting their home on fire and killing himself. It wouldn't be until months later that the town would learn that Scott had stolen millions in government money and was about to be exposed.

The people living in the small town couldn't fathom how life would ever seem normal again. But by the grace of God, working through people like Steve Frey, life would go on. And sometimes, as it is with most tragedies, even though the "why" may never be clearly understood, the love of God can still work miracles. Just ask Frey.

All of the events in Steve Frey's life led him to this particular day where he could serve as a healer to the young people in the community. This is not a tale of the infamous tragedy that took place in Platte in September of 2015; this is the story of Steve Frey's own personal journey and how all of the blessings and heartbreaks he'd experienced in his life, made him just the right person at the right time to teach others to trust and have faith, even when the unfathomable happens.

Little Brick in Platte, SD
Photo: Chad Phillips

Chapter 1: Alone & Broken Hearted

"Look to the right and see; for there is no one who regards me; There is no escape for me; No one cares for my soul." Psalm 142:4

Gone were the sunny, crisp fall days that usher in September, only to be replaced be the dull brown of November. That's the color of Thanksgiving in Iowa, from the ground to the trees to the sky. A brownish gray haze blankets the land. On this particular Thanksgiving — Nov, 22, 1979 — there was a sharp wind in the air that chilled Steve Frey to the bone as he walked with his head down toward the sleeping room he had rented in a rundown, old house in Monticello, Iowa. He had just finished the early morning wait shift at the truck stop, bringing plates of freshly scrambled eggs and sizzling bacon to tables filled with crusty drivers, who smelled of stale beer and cigarettes. The truck stop was located at the intersection of Highways 151 and 38, and it was closing at noon for the holiday.

Steve still felt hung over from the 12-pack he had guzzled when his shift at his other job, cutting hair at *Rod's Styling Bar*, had ended the evening before. He hadn't been drinking alone. There was always someone willing to drown their sorrows along with him. He tried to remember the name of the guy who drank with him the previous night outside of the liquor store in his beat-up 1970 Plymouth —*Bob? Rob? Ugh, something like that,* he sputtered. He wished he had a pair of gloves. His hands were cold and turning bright red. He made his way past the brick buildings downtown, which could have been in any Iowa town about the size of Monticello. As he rounded the corner, he approached the shabby home where he rented a room for $20 a week. The white paint on the siding was peeling, and one of the hinges on the screen door out front was broken, causing it to look off-kilter. He climbed the three wooden steps that had started to rot and pushed open the front door.

Inside it was dark and dingy. It was if the gray mist that enveloped the town that Thanksgiving Day had seeped in the entryway of the home and had swirled together with the feelings of hopelessness and dread that permeated every inch of the structure. The dark gloom rose up the rickety staircase, all the way to Steve's room. The weight of his poor decisions felt heavier and heavier on his shoulders as he climbed those stairs. He passed by the shared bathroom for all the tenants. It consisted of a basin sink, a toilet that was constantly plugged, a chipped white tile floor and a small, dingy shower stall with mold growing in the corners. The damp, musty smell filled Steve's nostrils and made him feel like gagging as he walked by the open door.

He walked by another door where he saw his neighbor, a tired-looking man of about 60 with grizzly, gray hair and a long beard. He was sitting on his bed, looking blankly at the wall in front of him. Steve had been told the older man's name was Earl, but the two had never so much as said "hello" to one another.

As Steve turned the cold metal knob on the door to his room, he felt a sense of trepidation sweep over him — a deep blackness that spread down to his very core. He shut the door to his room and looked around. The walls, which had once been white, had yellowed. There was a single bed in one corner. He never bothered to make it, and the sheets were dirty and tousled. On the small window across from the bed, there was a tattered shade, drawn down halfway to block out the muddy sky. There also was a well-worn armchair in the room and on it sat Steve's 22-caliber rifle. An older man, who had been an unlikely friend to Steve, had given him the gun long ago. But Steve wasn't thinking of the rifle's original owner right now or why he'd given it to him. Instead, as Steve looked at it, an idea that had been forming in the back of his mind for days, maybe even months, leaped to the surface with a jolt. *I'm a failure,* Steve thought. *A miserable, no good failure!*

Steve knew in his heart that he'd let everyone down, especially his four young children and his father. He imagined his family members sitting down for a big Thanksgiving meal right about now, only a few hours-drive away. *Did they even miss him? Where they relieved he wasn't there?* He approached the chair and picked up the rifle and carried it to his bed. He set the weapon gingerly on the bed and sank to his knees on the floor. Suddenly, the self-condemnation left his mind and his brain was flooded with a sense of relief. He didn't have to do this anymore! He could forever be rid of his self-imposed misery and suffering! *I'm ready*, he thought. *I'm ready to end it all.*

His hand began to shake as he reached toward the gun. The ticking of the large, wind-up alarm clock, on the little table next to his bed was the only sound that filled the room. But Steve didn't hear it anymore. The haze of the hangover had left him, and for the first time in nearly two years, Steve felt stone-cold sober. He knew what he had to do.

As his shaking fingers touched the barrel of the gun, he'd never felt more alone and broken-hearted. He picked it up and loaded 10 rounds of ammunition into the chamber. He had no one to blame but himself, and he knew it. Facing that truth felt like a sharp slap in the face. His trembling hands turned the gun over and with one hand he leaned it up toward his chest. The barrel was pointed toward his broken heart, pieces of which had scattered about like dried-up leaves. With his other trembling hand, he reached for the trigger.

Chapter 2: Rooted in Faith

"But as for you, continue in what you have learned and have become convinced of, because you know those from whom you learned it, and how from infancy you have known the Holy Scriptures, which are able to make you wise for salvation through faith in Christ Jesus." 2 Timothy 3:14-15

It was a Tuesday, but this was no ordinary day. On Sept. 26, 1950, when Steven Woodrow Frey was born, the sun turned a deep indigo blue, the same color as Steven's eyes. There was also a "blue moon" that night. The occurrence of both a blue sun and a blue moon was something that hadn't happened since a volcanic eruption nearly 70 years earlier. Scientists explained that it was caused by a scattering of light rays due to a strange breakdown of smoke particles from Canadian forest fires. But it just so happened that on that very same morning, the shadow of the earth darkened the moon, resulting in a lunar eclipse.

Steven came screaming into this world under those rare and mysterious astrological conditions, as the first and only son born to Berneice and Harley Frey in the tiny town of West Union, Iowa.

It was a simpler time. West Union is in the upper northeast corner of the Hawkeye State, and Harley Frey was a farmer. Harley had thick, dark brown hair. He stood 5 foot, 9 inches tall and was a stocky, but muscular 190 pounds. Harley got by on his looks and athletic prowess. Berneice was somewhat bookish, with brown hair, glasses and a soft-spoken manner. But if provoked, she could be quite feisty, which surprised those who didn't know her well. Berneice was brought up in the Christian church and told she should only marry someone who shared her deep faith. But she was crazy for Harley and felt lucky that he had chosen her from all the girls who had chased him. Harley reluctantly agreed to go to church with Berneice, even though he was an unbeliever. Shortly after they were married, after Berneice requested prayers from the congregation, Harley gave his life to Christ. Like everything else he set his mind to, he decided to become the best Christian possible, and he vowed to dedicate his life to spreading the Word of the Lord.

Harley Frey

Harley was an all-around athlete who seemed to easily excel at everything he did. Berneice had received her teaching degree from Luther College in Decorah, Iowa. But at the time Steve was born, she had given up teaching to become a farmer's wife. In the Frey household, Harley was boss; Berneice felt it was her job to keep the peace. She prided herself on having harmony in her home. She and Harley, who had married at age 19 and 21, respectively, were always affectionate with one another and made it a point to never argue in front of their four children. Janice was the oldest, followed by Diane, and 17 months later Steve, the only Frey boy, was born. Janice and Diane were so proud to sign their little brother's baby book. The youngest Frey child, Ruth, came along when Steve was six years old.

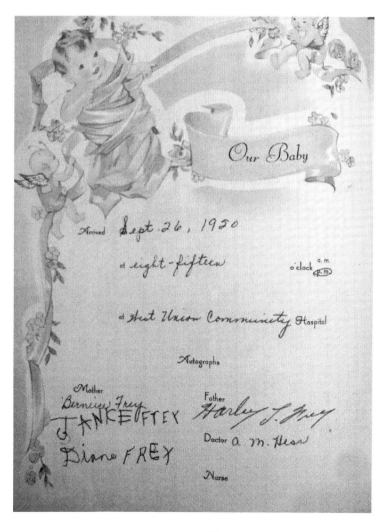

Janice, Steve & Diane Frey

Although he had entered the marriage as an unbeliever, when Steve was two, Harley felt called to the ministry and enrolled in the Lutheran Brethren seminary to become a pastor. He picked up his wife and the three children they had at the time and moved them to Fergus Falls, Minnesota, where they lived during the three-year program in cramped quarters in the dormitory. Ruth was born after Harley graduated from the seminary.

Harley's graduation from Lutheran Brethren Seminary, Fergus Falls, MN, 1956

Then Harley moved the family to Westby, Wisconsin, where he secured his first appointment as a pastor at Bethesda Lutheran Church. A town of about 1,500 people in 1956, Westby is best known for its three-day Syttende Mai festival, which celebrated Norwegian Independence Day. It was a Lutheran-potluck kind of town, where everybody knew everyone else and residents had Midwestern sensibilities; a no-nonsense kind of crowd. Harley was well received by the Scandinavians.

Bethesda church services were held in a basement. But Harley, who was a very persuasive man, convinced the parishioners to construct a full-fledged church above the basement. He did most of the work himself, stacking one log on top of the other to form the building. That log church is still in use today.

Harley's presence in that church was larger than life. He spoke to the congregation in the tradition of old-fashioned, Bible-thumping preachers of days gone by. He was gregarious and emotional, and his voice boomed throughout the church. Parishioners in the pews were convinced by his words. In fact, the congregation came up with an appropriate nickname for him: "Hollerin' Harley."

The Frey family

After moving to Westby, the Freys enrolled Steve in the first grade. Steve was only five when school started, but he would turn six a few weeks later. In those days, parents really didn't concern themselves about whether a child was ready for school. Steve was eligible to go, so his parents sent him. However, Steve, who was small for his age, was not prepared to enter a class of 30 students; he was terrified. This experience would mark the beginning of Steve feeling small and worthless. Harley always pushed his children to succeed, and Steve idolized his father and didn't want to let him down. But Steve felt even smaller than he was in stature and wished he could disappear right into the floor of that first-grade classroom. When the teacher, Mrs. Peterson, called on him, he shook in fear. He was so scared that he wet his pants, right in front of the entire class. Little Steve began to cry and turn bright red. He was humiliated. Steve had accidents at his desk caused by sheer terror several times during that first year of school.

A few weeks later, when Steve wet himself for the second time, Mrs. Peterson marched him the few blocks to the Freys' home and pounded on the door. When his parents answered she exclaimed, "He's done it again!"

Steve hung his head of dark hair, and his big blue eyes filled with tears as he wept in embarrassment. Berneice ushered him inside to change his clothes and sent him right back to school. Steve averted his eyes from everyone when he returned to the classroom. Several of his schoolmates pointed and taunted: "Baby! Baby wet his pants! Go home to mama, baby!"

Steve just stared at the ground and held back his tears. Those anxious and nervous feelings that began in first grade never dissipated for Steve. He carried them with him throughout his school years; constantly worrying that he would let his father down.

Steven Frey, First School Picture

One day in the second grade, Harley gave Steve a dollar to go get a haircut after school. Like a typical seven-year-old, Steve was distracted by the day's events in school and forgot all about it. He went skipping home from school, humming to himself. As soon as he entered the door of his house and stepped into the hallway, he encountered his dad.

"Steve, why didn't you get that haircut?" Harley demanded immediately.

"He wasn't there," Steve lied, referring to the barber. Steve looked down at his shoes. He was scared to tell him the truth, fearing Harley's disappointment in him.

"Well, then, tomorrow you'll go back!" Harley bellowed.

"Okay, okay," Steve mumbled.

Steve spent the next day, constantly reminding himself about that haircut and marched to the barber shop immediately after school. There was reason for Steve to fear his dad. Harley spanked Steve nearly every day when he was young. *Spare the rod and spoil the child,* was Harley's axiom. But that's not to say that Steve didn't bring even worse punishment on himself. His sisters Janice and Diane, who trembled in fear at the sound of Harley's thunderous voice, couldn't believe Steve's response when they saw him getting a whipping. Harley would say to him, "Are you going to behave?"

Steve would reply, "Yes, *but* ..."

That answer would only lead to another whipping, after which Harley would ask in an even louder voice: "Are you going to behave?" Then Harley would declare before Steve even had the chance to answer, "And no *buts* about it!"

However, after the beating, Harley would put Steve on his knee and say, "I love you so much." He would then instruct him in what he wanted him to do differently. Harley was a strict disciplinarian, but Steve truly believed, despite the pain his father inflicted on him, that he loved him.

The Bethesda Lutheran Church provided the family with housing, but the position didn't pay well and the family struggled to make ends meet. Steve saw a shiny silver pen in a shop in downtown Westby that he wanted. As most children will do, he begged and begged to get that pen. Steve was fixated on that pen and somehow got it in his head that that pen could make him a better student in school. Maybe it could even get him an "A" on his school work, instead of the usual "C," which was followed by the disappointed look on Harley's face that devastated Steve when he brought his assignments home.

After Steve endlessly pestered him for the money, Harley ordered from the living room to Berneice in the kitchen, "Berneice, go get my wallet!"

Berneice went into the other room and got Harley's wallet, and Harley took out the only dollar he had to his name.

"Steve, here you go. This is my last dollar, but it sounds like you need it more than I do," he said in a soft voice as he handed the bill to Steve.

Steve couldn't believe that his father actually gave in and gave him the money. Begging had rarely worked with Harley. Steve grabbed the dollar, clutched it tightly in his hand and took off on foot as fast as he could for downtown to buy that coveted pen, all the while knowing it was his father's last dollar. But about halfway to the shop, Steve stopped in his tracks. He was suddenly overcome by guilt as his conscious kicked in. Shame took hold of his stomach and crept into his throat. He marched back and handed the dollar to Harley. Harley was surprised his son had come home so quickly and was even more astonished when Steve held out that dollar bill.

"Here you go dad. I don't need that pen!" Steve exclaimed.

"Thank you, son. I'm proud of you for not being selfish. I love you, son," Harley said, beaming.

And while that may not seem like a big deal, the incident made a lasting impression on Steve. For the rest of his life he would remember that his father, when asked, was willing to give away his very last dollar.

One evening Harley called Janice outside.

"I want you to mow the lawn, Janice," Harley ordered. Janice was an athletic girl and Harley knew she was up for the job.

"I don't want to mow the lawn! What do I have a brother for?" Janice huffed.

"Okay, you don't have to mow the lawn, just go to bed, Janice," Harley said flatly.

Janice went up to her room and watched her father from her bedroom window as he mowed the yard. Janice stomach began to hurt and she was overcome by guilty feelings. Harley never spoke another word to her about it, but from that day on, Janice typically did what her father asked of her.

In order to support the family, Berneice worked as a nurse's aide on the overnight shift at the Westby Hospital. Harley drove the school bus, in addition to serving a pastor of the church. His booming voice kept the children on the bus in line, as he shuttled them to and from school. As the oldest, it was Janice's job to get all the children up in the morning, and Steve was the hardest to wake. Janice did all she could to get Steve up and off to school, from physically forcing him out of his bed to yelling at him to get up.

Janice complained to Harley, "I just can't get him up in the morning, Dad. He just makes it so hard!"

"Well," said Harley, "you just work on it and be nice,"

"I'm always nice, Dad!" professed Janice.

"I'll tell you what then," Harley said, pausing for a moment. "You try to get him up tomorrow morning, and if he won't get up, just let him sleep until I get home."

"Oh, yes," Janice thought. She could hardly wait to get her difficult little brother into trouble.

The next morning, she went into Steve's room and quietly whispered, "Steve, time to get up for school." Steve mumbled and rolled over, and all she could see was his head of dark hair. Janice left the room, smirking to herself, delighted at the thought of the punishment Steve likely would receive when their father got home. She wasn't disappointed. Harley put Steve over his knee and gave him a whipping with a wooden paddle. As Steve cried, Janice stood in the corner of the doorway. Pangs of guilt hit her like the flick of a rubber band, seeing the pain her pest-of-a-little-brother was going through. But at the same time, she was satisfied that the little troublemaker got what was coming to him. And, sure enough, that was the last time Steve overslept and was late for school!

Berneice would get home from the overnight shift at the hospital on Sunday mornings, and Harley would preach to the congregation on Sunday nights. Sunday afternoons were declared a quiet time for the family. Berneice and Harley took an afternoon nap, while they admonished the children to stay at home and entertain themselves. But they were told to remain *very* quiet. With no TV, video games or other forms of entertainment, the Frey children often played board games or told stories to one another. Diane and Steve, just 17 months apart in age, were close as small children. Sometimes Berneice even dressed them in matching outfits, as if they were twins.

Diane, Janice, Ruth & Steve

One Sunday afternoon, Janice decided that the four Frey kids should make taffy. It was great fun and difficult for the kids to keep quiet while they stirred sugar, cornstarch, butter and salt in a pan over the hot stove. They poured the hot mixture into a pan and then waited in anticipation for it to cool. Steve licked his lips, thinking of how sweet the candy would taste. Finally, it was time to pull the taffy into ropes, until it lost its shine and got stiff. Now this was the fun part! The three oldest Frey children began whipping the taffy ropes at one another. They all got horribly sticky, from head to toe, in the process. When Berneice woke up from her nap, much to her dismay, she found taffy strung all throughout the kitchen and hallway. Berneice was seldom the disciplinarian. That job was usually left to Harley. But this time, Berneice actually raised her voice.

"Children, what have you done?" she scowled. "Get this mess cleaned up right now!"

Janice, who had never seen her mother get this angry, looked down at the floor. Berneice handed each of her three children wet rags and ordered them to start scrubbing. For the next hour before church, Janice, Steve and Diane were down on their knees scouring the floors and walls of the kitchen and hallway. The incident made such an impression on Janice that she never again attempted to make taffy!

The people of Westby considered Harley Frey a great pastor, and he tried to pass along many of his Christian values to his children. In the late 1950s, communities often shunned people with developmental disabilities, and families typically hid them away in state mental hospitals. But Harley Frey taught his children that people with developmental disabilities were special and were put on this earth from God with a special purpose. He said their purpose here was to teach us how to love unconditionally.

One Saturday, when Steve was eight, he was riding his old, beat-up, hand-me-down, yellow bike along an Elm tree-lined street in Westby, when a developmentally disabled girl waved "hello" to him from the porch of a nearby home. Steve remembered his father's words about being kind to special girls and he knew he needed to say "hi" back. He looked over his shoulder to waive to the girl. But when he turned back around, his bicycle was headed straight for the curb. Steve desperately tried to correct his course and turned the handlebars, but the wheel didn't turn and it smacked right into the curb. The force propelled Steve over the top of the handlebars, bashing his testicles as his body lurched forward. He landed with a thud on the grass. By this time, the girl's parents were looking out from the porch and yelled over to him, asking if he was okay.

"I'm okay!" Steve yelled back, his face flushing with embarrassment. He flinched in pain as he got up and picked up his bike.

The front wheel was bent, so Steve grabbed the twisted handlebars and began walking the bicycle home. The Freys' home was just a few houses down the street from where the accident happened. As he pushed the bike along, Steve felt as if he'd wet his pants, again — just like in first grade. When he got back to the big, white, two-story home, he could hear his dad's resonant voice drifting out from the front parlor. As was his habit, Harley was singing a hymn, preparing for Sunday services the next day.

Steve headed up the stairs and went into the bathroom. Upon removing his pants, Steve discovered he was covered in blood from the waist down.

"*Ahhhhhh!*" Steve screamed. It was a scream loud enough to reach his father's ears as he sang out his song.

Harley came running into the bathroom and grabbed a towel and put it between Steve's legs. He picked up his son, put him in the backseat of the family's car and quickly drove him to the hospital. When they arrived, the doctor discovered that Steve had nearly cut off his testicles when he hit the handlebars. He was rushed into surgery, where the doctor was able to stitch him back up.

There was no more biking that summer. Instead, Steve had to lay on his back with ice packs on his privates — a tough way for an eight-year-old to spend his vacation from school. However, Steve suffered no permanent damage and, as an adult, went on to father four children. But when school started up that following year, he walked bull-legged into class. This provided his classmates with just one more reason to tease him — one more traumatic experience that would cultivate his insecurities.

In 1959, Harley was reassigned to a new parish: Bloom Prairie Church in Toronto, South Dakota, which had a population of about 300 people. Toronto is located in the far northeast corner of the state. The Frey family would live in Toronto through Steve's sophomore year of high school.

In Toronto, the students loved to play Carrom, a game imported from India. Carrom is a "strike and pocket" game like billiards. In Carrom, players use a stick to hit round, flat discs into the pockets of the board. Steve immediately made friends with boys who liked to play Carrom and while he was allowed to play the game with his friends, Harley told him he could not use a stick to strike the discs, because it reminded Harley of pool halls. Harley felt that pool halls were bastions of depravity and sin. While the other kids would use sticks to hit the Carrom discs, Steve had to flick them with his finger.

One time after school, Steve and three other boys pulled out the Carrom board in the classroom. They were all using sticks and when Steve's turn came up, one of the boys handed him the stick. He took it and began to make his shot, but then he looked up, and there stood Harley in the doorway to the classroom. His father immediately brought him home and gave him a beating. At nine, Steve began to feel like he was crumbling under the pressure to be perfect and could never live up to Harley's high expectations.

Being a preacher's child can be tough on kids; they often are held to higher standards than other children with less esteemed parents. Sometimes just being a typical kid and acting up in church could get Steve into serious trouble that had long-lasting consequences. It's tough for any nine-year-old boy to pay attention in church, even when your father is giving the sermon. During one Sunday service, Steve and his buddy, Gary Lenander, were goofing off in the back pew of the church, as Harley preached up front. Just as Harley's voice bellowed with Biblical stories about fire and brimstone and the redemption on the cross, out of the corner of his eye, he caught Steve whacking Gary with his fist, as Gary faked a grave injury. Suddenly Harley stopped mid-sentence.

"Steven Woodrow Frey!" Harley bellowed across the church.

"Oh man," Steve thought. *"Now I'm in trouble!"*

He knew it was a horrible sign when his dad had used his full name. Everyone in the congregation whipped their heads around to face the back of the church and all eyes were on him.

"Come up here, young man!" Harley ordered, sternly.

Steve felt his face burn hot and his feet were suddenly filled with lead. He reluctantly dragged his heavy limbs toward the front of the church.

"Yes, sir," Steve stammered, as he averted his eyes from his father. He could feel Gary's smirk on his back.

"You will sit right up front here, Steve — right here in the second row," Harley said demandingly as he pointed a stony finger to the edge of the pew to his right.

Steve took his seat as ordered. Harley continued with his sermon. Steve wished he could just melt into that pew.

It was customary for the family to have Sunday dinner together after the service and this day was no exception. On the car ride home, Steve sat in the back seat, thinking about the beating he was sure to get for his disrespect.

But instead of pulling out a paddle and ordering Steve to bend over his knee, Harley had something else in mind. As the Frey family gathered around their kitchen table, Harley turned to Steve and admonished him: "From now on, you will always sit in that spot in church, until I tell you to do otherwise."

Steve averted his eyes from Harley and nodded in agreement. He was just relieved he escaped the dreaded whipping. And every Sunday after that, Steve marched up to that second pew and sat down, as his father had instructed. Gary never even attempted to come up front to sit by him. A whole year passed before Steve got up the courage to ask Harley if he still had to continue to sit in that pew.

"Dad, I've been sitting there every Sunday for a year. I promise I won't be bad. I won't do anything wrong. I'll listen to your sermon. Can I *please* sit somewhere else? *Anywhere else*?" Steve pleaded.

"I'll tell you what, Steve," Harley acquiesced, staring intently at his son. "You may not sit anywhere else, but you can have your buddy, Gary, come sit up front with you." Harley said. He paused briefly, then added with a rising voice: "That's if you two can behave!"

Steve convinced Gary to join him in that second pew from the pulpit the following Sunday. And behave they did. Even though they looked stonily ahead, both boys were lost in their own thoughts rather than listening to Harley's sermon. Steve and Gary continued to sit in that same spot through their sophomore year of high school. And to all of the people in Toronto, Steve and Gary became known as the two boys who sat up front in church.

Steve's greatest goal as a teenager was to be as athletic as his father. But Steve was extremely short for his age. Harley coached Steve's baseball team and his thundering voice could be heard all across the ball diamond. Harley would declare to Steve, "A walk is as good as a hit."

Harley coaching Steve's baseball team in Toronto, Steve is in the second row, second from the left.

Janice, who was considered quite the tomboy, would spend hours helping Steve practice baseball — catching and throwing the ball outside of their home. Baseball wasn't the only sport that Steve played. He also was a member of the school's basketball team.

In 1964, when Steve was 14, the Toronto High School team played in the finals in White, South Dakota to qualify for the state basketball tournament. Even though he was still small in stature, Steve played his heart out to impress his athletic father. Toronto lost, but out of all the teams that played in that tournament, one player was given the sportsmanship award. Steve couldn't believe it when he heard his name announced over the gymnasium loud speaker: "And the sportsmanship award goes to Steve Frey!"

"I won? How could that be?" he thought.

As he made his way to the center of the gym to accept his award, he heard Harley bellow out, "That's *my* son!"

As he heard those words, Steve's heart swelled and he puffed out his chest. It was the one time in his life that Steve knew *for sure* that he had made his father proud.

"I'd rather have you win this award, than your team win the tournament," Harley proudly told Steve afterwards, with shining eyes and a huge smile beaming down at his son. Harley's approval meant so much to Steve that from that day on, Steve carried the small metal in his pocket wherever he went.

* * *

While Berneice wanted a peaceful home, there wasn't always harmony between the three older Frey siblings. Janice and Diane would chase Steve around the kitchen table during their rows. His sisters were relentless. One afternoon, after they tormented him endlessly, Steve went into the living room and sat on the recliner with a bag over his head. It was an effective strategy. His lack of response behind that paper bag caused his sisters to give up their campaign against him.

Steve with a paper bag over his head after a fight with his sisters

Sometimes Harley would witness these fights but would never interfere or stop Janice and Diane from torturing their little brother. Harley reasoned that Steve was the boy and should "man up," against his older sisters, who, granted, were still bigger and stronger than he was. Steve would get so angry with Janice and Diane that the veins on his forehead would bulge.

"I'm so mad I could just fly to the moon!" he'd holler.

Controlling his temper remained a difficult challenge for Steve for many years to come.

Late one fall, when Steve was 14, Harley and Berneice invited a group of Bloom Prairie parishioners to their home to partake in a Thanksgiving meal. Steve excused himself from the meal because he knew something was wrong. Upon further examination in the bathroom, he discovered that his torso was covered in welts.

Berneice, who had taken a job as a nurse's aide in Toronto, took one look at her son's mid-section and immediately took him to the doctor, where he was diagnosed with shingles. The doctor said the chickenpox virus and been reactivated in Steve's body because of his nerves. His sister, Diane, was in the same classroom as Steve and she'd witnessed how the teacher apparently disliked Steve, for no particular reason. The teacher's constant disapproval, along with his own, well-established anxieties, had taken their toll him.

When the doctor told Harley the reason Steve got shingles, Harley marched over to the school and he asked the teachers to be patient with Steve because he believed his son was on the verge of a nervous breakdown. While Harley didn't always come to Steve's defense, in this case he *was* protective of him. It was a difficult recovery for Steve. The pain was intense and the blisters broke open and soon crusted over. The pain gave way to terrible itching, and it took most of that school year until the blisters were gone.

During his freshman year of high school, Steve wrote a story in his English class. It was a lovely tale, set by a river, about a family of raccoons. Steve wrote about the mother raccoon feeding her babies. *"The young raccoons nestled in close to their mother as the moonlight glistened off the water,"* he wrote. Quite satisfied with his story, Steve marched up to the teacher's desk and handed in his paper, confident he would finally get an "A" and make Harley proud.

But much to his dismay, when the teacher returned his creative writing assignment a few days later in class, she had written a great big, fat "F" on his story about the family of raccoons. When Steve looked at her imploringly, the teacher went on to tell him that it *was too good for him to have written it.*

"There is no way you wrote this on your own, Steven," she said accusingly. "Where did you take this story from? I know you had to have copied it from somewhere!"

"Uh, uh," Steve stammered as his heart sunk. But before giving him a chance to defend his work, she turned and walked back up to the front of the classroom.

Steve shoved the paper in his textbook and dreaded going home that day. He knew that Harley would ask to look at his graded assignments. To his relief, this time, Steve did not get into trouble and Harley believed that his son had indeed written the beautiful and touching story. Harley was president of the Toronto School Board and used his influence to make sure that the teacher who had flunked Steve in English was let go at the end of the year.

Harley's influence was growing in the region. He was responsible for getting schools in the communities of White and Toronto to consolidate. The new Deubrook School District could share its resources and save tax money. That feat got Harley named Citizen of the Year in Brookings County, South Dakota.

While Harley was well known and well respected in White, South Dakota, he was still barely making a living on his pastor's salary. Everyone was expected to pitch in to help clothe and feed the five family members. Harley found Steve a used bicycle and fixed it up, and then built a trailer with two wheels that could be attached to the bike. The family had a large garden tended by Steve's mother and sisters. Every summer, Steve loaded the bicycle trailer with squash, rode around town, and sold them for five cents apiece.

One summer, Harley bought Steve a gas-powered lawnmower, which at $45 was a lot of money in those days.

He announced to Steve, "This is the last lawn mower I'm ever going to buy you."

Steve put a sign up in the Toronto grocery store to advertise his services. He mowed lawns all summer for a dollar apiece. Steve wrote down all the lawns he mowed in a notebook to keep track of them. At the end of the season, Harley and Steve would total it all up. Steve would then use the money to buy savings bonds. Steve never complained about doing the odd jobs and credited Harley with teaching him a strong work ethic at a young age.

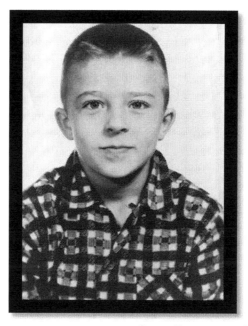

Steve Frey at age 8

Two blocks away from the Freys' Toronto home was a ramshackle house that was practically falling down. The weeds out front were waist high. The owner of the shack was Julius Miner. Julius had only one leg and used a wheelchair. Most of the kids in Toronto made up stories about why Julius had only one leg. They were all scared to death of him, but that didn't stop a kid or two from throwing rocks at his windows. Julius just lived with the broken panes of glass, even when the bitter air from the South Dakota winters made their way inside. There was no running water in the shack, and it was filthy. Dirty dishes and cups piled high on the counters.

Harley told Steve that he was to go to Julius' house one summer and become his friend. "Every day, you'll take him a newspaper," Harley ordered,

"Okay," Steve muttered, with his head down. He wasn't about to tell his father he didn't want to go into that creepy old house. Steve slowly dragged his feet during the two-block walk to Julius' house and knocked on the door.

"Come in," croaked a hoarse, gravelly voice from inside.

Steve warily pulled the door open and peered inside. He spotted Julius in the corner in his wheelchair with his bushy, unkempt hair, bulging eyes and a stump where his leg should have been. Julius sat as upright as he could in the chair when he saw Steve.

"What do you want, boy," Julius growled, figuring Steve was there to torment him or play a trick on him, as other boys in town had done.

"I'm Harley Frey's son," Steve uttered tautly, looking around the shack at the mess of the man and his grimy surroundings. "He asked me to bring you this newspaper."

"Well then," Julius sighed, visibly softening. "Come here, boy, and give it to me!"

Steve gingerly made his way around the debris on the floor to Julius and shoved the newspaper toward him. Julius took the paper, set it on the small table next to him and then rustled around in his wheelchair, turning to grab a dirty drinking glass off the counter nearby. Flies buzzed everywhere in the dark room, even touching down on the glass Julius held in his hand.

"Grab that grape juice over there, boy!" he ordered, pointing at a dirty pile on the table close to Steve. Steve did as he was told.

"Now pour some of that into this glass and sit down and take a load off! Have some juice. I've got something to show you!"

Steve's stomach did cartwheels, just thinking about drinking the warm grape juice out of the dirty glass. But he pulled up a chair next to Julius, dusted it off, and sat down with the glass of juice. Reluctantly, he brought it to his lips. He remembered Harley telling him to be polite and to take what people offered him.

"Come on, boy, drink up!" Julius bellowed.

And with that, Julius whipped out a harmonica he had tucked next to his good leg in his wheelchair. He pursed his lips and began to play. Steve couldn't believe his ears. Oh, the way that Julius could make the harmonica sing! And all the while,

Julius' stump flopped up and down, up and down, up and down to the beat.

Every day for the next three summers, Steve brought Julius his newspaper, and Julius played the harmonica for him. A bond of friendship was formed. A few years later, after he'd long since left Toronto, Steve got a call from Harley.

"Julius died," Harley whispered. "But he left you something — the only thing of value that he owned — his 22-rifle. You were his only friend."

Steve came to treasure that gun, knowing how much it meant to Julius. He vowed to never forget the lesson his dad was teaching him: how to love people unconditionally, just as God does. Unfortunately, later on Steve would go through such difficulties that the significance of Julius' gift would be lost on him; he forgot that God's love also applied to him.

* * *

The following spring, Harley had taken on a big project. He was plumbing the basement so the family could have another bathroom. One evening after supper, Steve found his father hard at work,

"Hey Dad, can I go uptown to the ball game?" Steve asked.

"I need your help down here with this plumbing," Harley told him.

So, Steve began to help his dad and after a while, they completed the project.

"Now can I go to the game?" Steve implored.

"No," Harley said, sighing.

Steve couldn't believe what he was hearing. He had done everything Harley had asked. He felt his face growing hot. Most of his friends were at the game. *Their dads didn't make them work first,* Steve thought angrily.

"But, Dad," Steve said, beginning to protest.

"I want to see if you can take no for an answer. When you can learn to help somebody without asking for something in return, then you're a man," Harley lectured.

Steve shook his head and went back upstairs, muttering protests under his breath.

It was always a test with his father, Steve thought, a test to see if he would become the kind of man his father was — a test he would eventually fail in the worst of all possible ways.

One day, while the family was still living in Toronto, Harley called the three Frey children into the living room.

"You're all going to have to be much nicer to your mother," he pleaded, looking as if he were about to cry.

"What's the matter?" they rang out in unison. The Frey children had never seen Harley looking so despondent. They could never imagine their larger-than-life father ever appearing weak.

"All you need to know," Harley replied sternly, "is that your mother is not going to be home for a while. "

It was years later that Steve learned his mother had a nervous breakdown. The family never spoke of Berneice's hospital stay or the issues she faced.

"She just isn't feeling well," Harley told the children when Berneice came home from the Hendricks, Minnesota hospital a month later.

Steve figured his mother had suffered from the flu and everything pretty much went back to normal. Harley never confided in anyone about Berneice's breakdown — after all, she was the minister's wife and had a reputation to uphold. The older he got, the more Steve realized he had inherited some of his anxiety and depression issues from his mother.

The Frey family

Chapter 3: Leaving Home

"How can a young man keep his way pure? By keeping it according to Your word. With all my heart, I have sought You; do not let me wander from Your commandments." Psalms 119-9-10

After Janice's sophomore year, she left Toronto to go Hillcrest Lutheran Academy in Fergus Falls, Minnesota. Janice would complete her junior and senior years at the boarding school, and Diane followed in her older sister's footsteps.

At the end of Steve's sophomore year, the Frey family moved again. Harley Frey had accepted a new position as pastor of the Lutheran Church in Crosby, North Dakota. Steve assumed he would be going to Hillcrest Lutheran Academy, just as his sisters had done. After spending the summer back at his grandparents' home in West Union, Iowa, Steve asked his dad, "Will I be going to Hillcrest?"

"No," Harley replied in a firm, even tone. "You're not mature enough."

Steve hung his head. While he desperately sought his father's approval, at that moment, he knew as the only son, he was not living up to the man his father wanted him to be. He didn't know how he ever could.

But Steve was soon to take on a more adult role. Once they got back to Toronto, the family prepared to move to North Dakota. A member of the Lutheran Church in Crosby came down to Toronto in a farm truck and loaded the Freys' furniture in it. At his parents' urging, Steve jumped in the truck with the stranger and rode up to Crosby, which is just six miles south of the Canadian border. Steve lived with the man and his wife for two weeks, until the rest of the family arrived in Crosby. Sending a child hundreds of miles away with a stranger is something no parent would dream of doing today, but it was a much more trusting time, especially in small communities. However, with 1,700 residents in 1966, Crosby was nearly three times larger than Toronto.

Steve attended the Crosby High School his junior year, and he took a job working at the Red Owl grocery store in town. The summer after his junior year, the Red Owl in Plentywood, Montana, which was 35 miles away, needed some help. So Berneice and Harley allowed Steve to drive over to Plentywood and live in a hotel for a month at 16 years of age. But he didn't want to go back to the Crosby High School his senior year. He continued to pester Harley about attending Hillcrest in Fergus Falls. Finally, he wore Harley down.

"Okay, okay," Harley reluctantly told Steve. "You're going to Hillcrest your senior year."

After his stint working in the Montana Red Owl store, Steve packed up for the Minnesota boarding school. Steve was 17 and would never live at home with his parents again. While he couldn't wait to get to Hillcrest, his enthusiasm was about to sour. The 250 students came from all over the United States, as far away as New York and Chicago. It didn't take long for Steve to realize that he was one of the poorest students attending the private Lutheran boarding school. His sisters, Janice and Diane, had both helped earn their tuition money by working in the school's kitchen. One day, he picked up the phone and called his parents,

"Do you have any money at all?" he whined.

Harley reluctantly replied, "I'll send you some money, son."

A week later, Steve received $5 in the mail. But $5 wasn't enough for Steve to buy the popular Pendleton's shirts that all his classmates were wearing. The short-sleeve, wool, button-down shirt cost $13.95. Tuition for Hillcrest was $1,000 a year, and in 1967 that was lot of money. Harley Frey didn't get any kind of break on the fee, even though he was a Lutheran pastor. The money Steve had earned working so hard

Steve Frey at Hillcrest, third row from the bottom, second in from the right

at the Red Owl, as well as his savings bonds that he purchased with his mowing money, all went toward his tuition.

On the first day he arrived on campus, Steve wanted to try out for football. He was told practice was underway, so he ran down to the field, and put his pads and helmet on. While Steve got to campus before school started, the team had arrived a week earlier for football practice. Steve was undeterred and practiced with the team, although he hardly got any time on the field. Afterward, the coach admonished him. "Steve, you're a week late," the coach told him. "We've got the team roster sent in to the Minnesota State High School Activities Association. Don't go out. We're not going to have you play that much anyway."

Steve's heart sank. He was crushed but continued to try to figure out how he could fit in at this new school.

Basketball season arrived, and Steve planned to play. Even though he was short at just 5 foot, 8 inches, he'd played at other schools in South Dakota and North Dakota, and he loved the game. He showed up at the Hillcrest Gym for the first day of practice and the same coach was heading the team.

"Steve," he called him over. "You're a senior. We've already got the team set."

And just like that, without even getting a chance to get

Steve Frey Senior Picture

on the court, Steve was cut from the Hillcrest team. Steve was discouraged and felt like there was no place for him to fit in at Hillcrest. And to make it even worse, not a single girl would even look his way. Short, unpopular and poor, he didn't measure up to the big jocks on campus. He knew he'd never get a girlfriend at this rate.

But late in his senior year, there was a girl — one girl— who actually spoke to him. Her name was Marlene Luckey, and she was a year behind him in school. Marlene was a slight girl — about 5 foot, 6 inches tall — with long, straight brown hair. There was nothing that really stood out about Marlene; in fact she blended in with all the rest of the girls. But Marlene actually gave Steve a shy smile as she passed him in the hallway at school. And occasionally she would sit with him and a group of other students in the cafeteria during lunch. Steve was craving attention and took the scraps Marlene threw his way to heart. But he would be graduating soon, and she still had an entire year to go. So he didn't ever ask her out on a date. Even though he was earning "Ds" and "Cs," in his classes, he managed to get his diploma. He was only 17.

Steve and a classmate at Hillcrest graduation

Following graduation, Steve went to West Union, Iowa to visit some Frey relatives and work at the family's dairy. The dairy farm also included a restaurant and was known all around the area for its ice cream. Steve was trying to figure out what to do next, when he saw his favorite uncle, with whom he shared a middle name. Glen *Woodrow* Frey had been pleased when his brother and sister-in-law decided to name their only son, Steven *Woodrow* Frey. When Glen saw Steve that summer following high school, he suggested his namesake also take on his profession.

"Why don't you become a barber?" Glen asked Steve one day when he saw him at the dairy. "I think you'd be really good at that," Glen told him.

The next time Steve talked to Harley on the phone he told him about the idea.

"I think you could probably do that," Harley agreed, flatly.

While it wasn't much, that was all the encouragement Steve needed to enroll at Barber College in Waterloo, Iowa in August 1968.

It wasn't Steve's lifelong dream to become a barber, but he figured he might as well walk in his uncle's footsteps. After all, he didn't have a better plan. Steve found a room to rent in Waterloo for $6 a week. It was in one of the poorest areas of town. On Sept. 13, 1968 race riots broke out in Waterloo after police tried to arrest an African American man outside of a high school football stadium during a game between an all-white school and all-black school. Fires were set, and violence erupted. In the end, seven police officers were hurt and 13 people were arrested. The National Guard was called in to keep the peace the following day.

For the first time in his life, Steve experienced racial tension. Until this point, he hadn't even encountered any black people at all in the tiny South Dakota and North Dakota towns he lived in, or at the Lutheran high school in Minnesota.

One day, while walking home from Waterloo Barber College to his rundown rental room, a car with four young black men pulled up next to him. They began yelling profanities at Steve and threatened him. He was terrified. Steve took off running as fast as he could, cutting through yards and alleyways as the men continued to chase him.

"Hey, whitey," they screamed from the windows. "We're going to f@##ing kill you! You'd better run!"

After about 10 blocks, as he arrived at his building, they caught up to him. He ran for the door, and the men continued to yell from the vehicle, threatening to beat him to death. But the men did not try to follow him inside.

Not only did Steve feel unsafe in Waterloo during those tumultuous times, he was also hungry. There was one week, where all he was able to afford was a case of 7UP, three cans of peas and some popcorn. Growing up, he'd never felt the kind of hunger pains that he experienced while in barber school. He was so desperate and broke that after getting a ride to West Union for the weekend, he stole food from the restaurant his aunt and uncle ran at the family dairy. Months later, his Aunt Ercyle was dying from breast cancer. Ercyle, who had once been a vibrant woman, was thin and weary. Steve arrived at her bedside, knelt down and confessed his sin.

"Aunt Ercyle, I need your forgiveness."

Ercyle looked at him with compassion as he described what he had done.

"Steve, you are forgiven. Don't ever mention it again," she declared in a weak voice. It was among the last words she would utter.

Years later, Steve told his Uncle Kenneth, Ercyle's husband, about that moment of forgiveness on Ercyle's deathbed.

"She died forgiving you," Kenneth told him. "She never told a soul. I had no idea."

Ercyle's forgiveness left a lasting impression on Steve; one that later helped him get through difficult time.

Steve was lonely during his time in Waterloo. He longed for a girlfriend, and he remembered Marlene Luckey from back at Hillcrest. Steve had asked for her address when he left school. One night after returning from class at Barber College, he sat down and wrote her a letter:

Hi, this is Steve Frey. Do you remember me?

He didn't write much else that was interesting. He described his classes and how he was learning to cut hair and what the town of Waterloo was like. He left out being chased by the carload of African American men. He dropped the letter in the post box and was thrilled two weeks later, when she wrote back. Marlene was living at home with her parents and going to a junior college in Littleton, Colorado. It was the first of 10 letters — mostly just documenting how each spent their days — that the two would exchange over the next year.

At age 18, Steve completed Barber College in Waterloo. He took his first job working for a Main Street barber in Sheffield, Iowa, near Mason City. The owner of the barbershop, Ron Hite, took Steve under his wing. Steve earned 25 cents for every shave and 75 cents per haircut. He managed to take home about $30 a week. He found another young man, a teacher named Dennis Brinkman, to share a small apartment. The year was 1969, the first year a lottery drawing for the military draft had been reinstated since 1942.

Steve, Dennis and a few other guys gathered around the TV on December 1st for the nationally televised drawing of the draft. After just 10 minutes, Steve's number, 18, was picked. The party was over. He was going to Vietnam. He was going to war.

Chapter 4: Vietnam Years

"And when you go to war in your land against the adversary who oppresses you, then you shall sound an alarm with the trumpets, that you may be remembered before the LORD *your God, and you shall be saved from your enemies."* Numbers 10:9

A short time later, Steve's draft letter from the government arrived in his mailbox. Many draft dodgers were choosing to flee to Canada instead of going to Vietnam. Others enrolled in college as quickly as possible to avoid the draft. A million things were going through Steve's mind. He didn't know what to do. *Should I run away?* He thought. *How would I get to Canada?* He picked up the rotary phone in his tiny apartment kitchen and dialed Harley's number.

"Dad, my draft letter came in the mail," Steve lamented, his voice shaking. "What do I do?'

"I know one thing you don't do, Steve," Harley proclaimed over the line, as it crackled. There was a long pause. Steve waited for his father's reply, but in his heart, he already knew what Harley would say.

"You need to do what's right, son. The Frey men are honorable. You will not run away from this."

"What should I do then?" Steve whimpered.

"I'll tell you what you do. You go down to the recruiting station and enlist. And sign up for an extra year. Then maybe you can save your life." Harley advised sternly.

The young men who enlisted typically had more of a choice in their assigned job in the military. It was the only thing that could possibly save Steve from the front lines of battle with the Viet Cong in the jungles of Vietnam.

"Okay, thanks, Dad. That's what I'll do," Steve answered.

That afternoon, Steve drove to Mason City, Iowa, marched into the recruiter's office and enlisted. The Army recruiter handed him a ticket for a Greyhound bus to Des Moines. Steve's sister, Diane, was attending North Iowa Area Community College in Mason City as the time. Steve called his sister and told her that he had enlisted and that he would be leaving town for basic training the following day.

Diane hopped on a city bus the next morning to see Steve off at the Mason City bus terminal. In the days of the Vietnam War, there were no formal military send-offs for families of new recruits, such as the ceremonies held for today's military members when they're called up to serve. While Diane and Steve had often been at odds as children, Steve looked into his sister's eyes and could see the concern. Everyone knew somebody who had never made it back from Vietnam.

Diane reached up and tousled Steve's hair. "Take care of yourself, little brother!" she insisted, endearingly.

Steve shrugged and bit his lip, trying to fight back tears. Then, impulsively, Diane threw her arms around him and hugged him. It may have been the most affection she'd ever shown for her annoying little brother, who she always felt was their father's favorite. That was something that Steve could never see. As she let go of him, the bus pulled up to the curb. Steve looked down so Diane couldn't see the tears forming in his eyes.

"You too, sis," he requested. "Don't get into any trouble while I'm gone," he continued, lifting his head to give her a half smile.

Steve & Diane when he left for the army

Then he climbed up the steps of waiting Greyhound. He maneuvered his way into a window seat and looked down below at Diane, who raised her hand in a wave, tears streaking down her face. Steve pressed his hand against the glass and then adjusted the duffle bag in his lap. With all the stops the Greyhound made along the way, it was a four-hour bus ride to Des Moines.

Steve and several other young men disembarked the bus at the Iowa National Guard Armory on the south side of Des Moines. Over the next several hours, some 500 men filled the military installation. Even though other young men surrounded him who were all in the same boat — facing the same uncertain circumstances — Steve had never felt more alone. They were herded like cattle inside the large building and ordered to line up, 50 men per line. Rows of young men, who looked more like boys right off Iowa farms, stood shoulder to shoulder as a male medic, dressed in green fatigues, walked up to each one, and stuck a wooden tongue depressor down his throat.

As they stood there side-by-side, a drill sergeant barked out orders: "Ten Hut! Drop your pants! Do it now! Pants down! Shorts down! Bend over! Grab your ankles!" barked the drill sergeant, who was flanked by two corporals. The corporals had swagger sticks hanging from their belts as they walked the lines.

The young men glanced hesitantly at one another. They hadn't expected this. But one by one they each did as they were ordered. Steve bent over and could see the backs of the heads of the 50 men in the line behind him doing the same.

"Now spread your cheeks! That's what I said, spread them now!"

Another officer had started at one line, walking behind each man and shoving his finger up their anuses, looking for hemorrhoids. Or at least that's what Steve figured they had to be doing. It was just the start of the indoctrination that the men would endure as they became U.S. Army soldiers. It seemed surreal to Steve that this could be happening, as he felt the cold, rubbery finger of one of the corporals penetrate him from behind. Then, from ahead of him, came a huge, loud, long fart, breaking the tension, as the young men all started laughing.

"Attention!" Quiet you little f *#@*ers!" the drill sergeant shouted. And he began to call them every name in the book.

Steve, who had been raised in a Christian home, where this kind of language would never have been permitted, had never heard most of the profanities. He found it hard to get over his shock and he wondered if the sergeant was a Christian. *With language like that, how could he be?* Steve thought.

Then another corporal in Army greens passed out plastic cups and they were all told to urinate in them, right there in front of everyone. Steve looked around. *Was he going to be able to produce any pee at all?* He felt more like throwing up than urinating. But he managed to get a little stream into the cup. Each of the enlisted men were then handed a piece of paper with their name on it. Steve took his paper from the corporal and began to make his way inside the building as the sergeant barked out more orders. As the men moved toward the building, their cups of pee in hand, some began to snicker and laugh. One enlistee had defecated right into his cup. But this wasn't just an attempt to get a laugh. Many of those drafted were trying to claim they were mentally unstable. From mental illness to bad eyesight to bad hearing, they tried any excuse to avoid being shipped off to war.

After depositing their urine in the building, they were fed and then led into the barracks, where they all fell into their bunks exhausted. But it was a short night. A whistle sounded over the loudspeaker at 4 a.m.

"Ten hut!" the voice of the drill sergeant from the day before came barreling over the loudspeaker. "Attention you a#%holes!"

Steven rubbed his eyes and rolled out of bed. He made his way to the end of the bunk. A corporal was walking through the barracks, handing each man his assignment on a piece of paper. Steve gingerly took his small piece of paper and peered at the words on it. It read, "Fort Lewis, Washington." The sleepy men stumbled out of the barracks and were directed to the military planes waiting outside in the airfield. Steve boarded the plane with 100 other men, headed for Washington State.

When they arrived at Fort Lewis, the men once again lined up in the barracks and another corporal, who seemed just like the last one in Des Moines, passed out a cardboard box to each one. He ordered them to take off their civilian clothes and put them in the box, and put their next of kin's name and address on the box. They all stripped down and Steve began to put his clothes in the box. Then he wrote Harley's and Berneice's names and their North Dakota address on the box. Each man was handed white boxer shorts and an undershirt, along with green fatigues. They each received Army green shirts, green belts and socks and black combat boots. They then were told to stand in line. The next step was a haircut. Steve went inside the small building and sat down in the chair.

"How do you want this cut?" the Army private asked him sarcastically.

Steve upper lip began to curl. He knew his response didn't matter. He'd seen every guy that walked in the building come out the other door with a shaved head. He stared straight ahead as the private moved the razor across his thick, dark hair. Out of the corner of his eye, he watched his hair fall onto the ground. When the private was done running the razor over his head, Steve barely recognized himself.

He made his way back outside to stand in line with other newly enlisted men. They all looked identical with their green fatigues and shaved heads. The sergeant ordered them to stand at "parade rest," with their hands behind their backs. As they stood there, an hour turned into two hours, and that turned into three hours and then four. It began to rain. Steve silently began to cry, his tears blending in with the raindrops on his face. He longed for home. He pictured Harley's face in his mind and his body shook slightly. No one said a word, but Steve could hear the sounds of other men sobbing.

Tired, wet and hungry, they were eventually dismissed to their barracks and assigned a bunk. As Steve made his way to his bed, he watched as many of his comrades sat on the edge of their bunks, crying like babies, each imagining how they were being sent to their untimely deaths in Vietnam. They were still boys, in so many ways, but they were being forced to grow up fast now. Steve realized he didn't feel like crying any more as he settled into his bunk. Perhaps Harley's tough lessons growing up had all been for this purpose; he felt a strength he didn't know he possessed. He'd been beaten down and survived before.

He wasn't going to quit. I am going to make it through basic training. I am not going to fail and go home in disgrace, Steve thought as his jaw hardened. At that moment, Steve vowed that he would be strong and finally make Harley proud.

Tensions were running high in the barracks the next day. Steve was making his way toward the shower, when he heard shouting. A fight had broken out between two of the enlistees. Steve watched as a burly young man from Wisconsin named Lenny swung a punch at a smaller man from Virginia, named Rob, and hit him right in the mouth. The other men in the barracks began shouting, egging them on. Amid the chaos, in burst two corporals. They dragged Lenny out through the barracks, buck-naked. Steve didn't see him return.

The following day, as the privates lined up for drills, the sergeant began to verbally assault them with every name in the book. Then he ordered: "Look over there, you, f*#@ing losers, you miserable pathetic excuses for men!" he barked as he pointed his finger toward a nearby field.

The men all turned their heads in the direction the sergeant was pointing. And there on the ground, in the sandpit, was Lenny with a sandbag tied to each arm. Two corporals stood above him, forcing him to low crawl on his stomach 100 yards. The corporals got down in his face and screamed at him, forcing him on. You could see the look of shock in the faces of the privates who silently watched the horrible scene unfold. They knew at that moment what their fate would be if they made such a mistake.

The rest of the men continued with their maneuvers, running 20 miles through the heavily wooded and hilly area that made up the base at Fort Lewis. Seven hours had passed while they underwent drills. As the men made their way back to camp, rain started to pour down. As they approached the barracks, they saw Lenny still lying on the ground in the sandpit, where he had been crawling when they left. They couldn't tell if he was dead or alive. And that was the scenario that played out, day after day, as the men were made into soldiers. Two weeks went by, and every day Lenny was out crawling in the sandpit as the officers verbally assaulted him.

"I want to go to Vietnam! I want to kill the Charlie Kong," Steve and the other privates chanted as they marched. Steve could feel a hardness entering his heart. He knew that from this moment on he would never be the same. He felt a sense of loss as his youthful optimism slipped away.

"Eyes right," the sergeant ordered.

All of the privates turned their heads to the right and looked at the sandpit where Lenny had spent hours, day after day, crawling on his belly. But it was empty. Lenny was gone.

"Suckers, that loser Lenny finally graduated. Now, the next one of you who wants to volunteer to take his place in the sandpit, step up to the front!" the sergeant hollered.

All of the privates looked stonily ahead. Steve wondered if Lenny had died.

"That's what I thought," the sergeant bellowed after none of the soldiers volunteered.

That night, back in the barracks, all the men were asking each other if anyone knew what had happened to Lenny. A skinny redheaded kid named Joe, from Montana, told the rest of them that he had seen Lenny marching with a different company. You could almost hear the collective sigh of relief across the room as the privates heard that Lenny had survived his torment and had been transferred.

As part of the basic training, Steve and his fellow privates were taken to a clearing in the woods on base. Several poles reaching some 50 feet in the air stood about 10 feet apart, with ropes in between each one. The series of polls connecting the ropes to one another created a sky-high obstacle course. Steve looked up at the towering wooden beams and shuddered. He knew what was coming next, and he wasn't sure he could do it. As long as he could remember, Steve had been afraid of heights. He remembered Harley asking him to climb up one of the church towers to adjust the bell and he just couldn't do it. He began crying and shaking as Harley stood below, urging him to go higher. When Harley saw how traumatized Steve had become, he told him to come back down and went up himself. That incident came flashing back to him now as he looked up at the ropes above him.

Steve's eyes followed the ropes and 20 yards away were two more poles.

"Ten hut! Up the ropes on these poles, privates! Across the ropes and back down the ropes on the other side!" the drill sergeant ordered. "Single file. Now go!"

Steve watched as the most athletic privates began scurrying up the ropes, dangling from the poles as if it were the easiest thing to do in the world. They grabbed the ropes on top and swung like monkeys to the next pole, back across another rope and down the final rope hanging from the fourth pole. The line moved rapidly, as the sergeant ordered them to go faster. A chubby private from Chicago, who stood four men in line ahead of Steve, struggled to hoist himself up on the rope on the first pole. He could barely get off the ground. The line slowed down. The drill sergeant ordered him off.

"Look who can't make it up the pole! Fat little Freddie here can't do it! We call Fatty here 'Girly' from now on, boys! Girly, get down and give me 50!" the sergeant screamed.

The drill sergeant stood over the chunky private who began doing pushups, but struggled after just 20 of them. Steve thought to himself, *I'm not going to be like him!* As the sergeant continued screaming at the private from Chicago, the line began moving again, as more men made their way up the pole. Steve's turn arrived. His stomach was churning and sheer terror gripped him. He closed his eyes as he made his way up the rope on the first pole. At the top, he looked through slanted eyes at the ropes, grabbing the ones in front of him and closing his eyes tightly again. He grabbed the ropes, one hand in front of the other, now again, and again.

"Faster, Frey, faster, you #$***$%!" the drill sergeant screamed from below, assaulting him with swear word after swear word.

This is a test that I will not fail! Steve thought. The ropes were swaying and swinging under his grip. He felt dizzy, but failure was not an option. He held on for his life and grabbed for the next rope, one after the other. With solid determination, he made it all the way around the ropes to the last pole. Now he had to climb down the rope on the other side. He looked down for a moment, to grab the correct rope and thought he would faint. He took a deep breath, grabbed the final rope and began shimmying his way down. As his feet hit the ground, Steve couldn't believe he had done it, but he had! He had overcome his fear and passed this test.

Another test facing the new soldiers was the gas chamber. The chamber was 10 feet wide, 10 feet long and totally dark. The young men were equipped with gas masks and ordered inside the building. Tear gas filled the room, and the sergeant barked out orders. "Gas masks off!"

The men took off their masks, their eyes watering, as the gas descended upon their lungs, suffocating them. One by one they shouted out their names.

"Private E1 Steven Woodrow Frey" Steve choked out, followed by his Social Security number.

The drill sergeant stood before him with his mask securely on. "Okay, go!" the sergeant said in a muffled voice through his own mask.

Steve walked out of the chamber as quickly as possible and vomited on the ground, right outside the door, along with a couple dozen other men who were hunched over wrenching. Their skin burned and itched as the chemical penetrated their clothing. But they had to continue with drills for the rest of the day. If anyone was caught itching his skin, he had to drop to the ground and give the sergeant another 20 pushups. Steve would experience the gas chamber training three times while he was in the military.

Steve Frey is fourth row down from the top, third from the left, wearing glasses

Chapter 5: There but for the Grace of God, Go I

"But by the grace of God I am what I am: and his grace which was bestowed upon me was not in vain; but I labored more abundantly than they all: yet not I, but the grace of God which was with me." 1 Corinthians 15:10

Steve and his fellow privates completed basic training in eight weeks. The Army then gave the new soldiers their marching orders. Some soldiers would be shipped out to Fort Hood, Texas, where their "tickets would be punched" for Vietnam almost immediately. Steve held his breath as the corporal handed him his orders: *Steven Woodrow Frey: Fort Ord, California,* it read. Steve let out a long sigh of relief. Soldiers at Fort Ord were not being sent to Vietnam at that time.

After arriving at Fort Ord, the Army put Steve through more training maneuvers, but they didn't seem as difficult to him as they were at Fort Lewis. Maybe he was just getting stronger. A short drill sergeant of Japanese descent was in charge of the company. He stood before the men and began to yell. "Attention you losers, you *blankety, blank, blank* good for nothing SOBs!"

He began to turn red in the face. The privates began to smirk at the site of the sergeant, so small in stature and now nearly turning purple. "You are the sorriest group of a-holes I've ever seen!"

"That's me. I'm the biggest one," a private named Henry mumbled under his breath.

"Get down and give me 20," the sergeant ordered angrily and the men all began doing pushups, as ordered.

A couple of guys struggled to do them, making the sergeant even hotter. "You such a sorry bunch of a-holes, even my a-hole bleeds for you!" he raged.

That caused the privates to break out into laughter, which only earned them more pushups. It became a vicious cycle, the more the sergeant barked out profanities and insults, the more the young men snickered and the more pushups they had to do.

At Fort Ord, Steve was assigned to Advanced Individual Training, or AIT. That meant that in addition to running drills, he attended classes. Steve was supposed to learn to type, but he never did quite master that skill.

One evening after he had arrived on base, Steve went to the enlisted men's club. He was walking by a table when one of the privates seated there said, "Hey, Frey!"

Steve couldn't believe it. There sat a group of guys he knew from his junior year in high school in Crosby, North Dakota.

"Hey, you guys heading for Vietnam?" Steve asked.

"No way," they retorted.

"What are you guys doing here then?' Steve asked.

"You remember David Elsbernd from our class in Crosby?" One of the guys questioned.

"Sure," Steve replied.

"Well, he was killed in Vietnam and so we all joined the National Guard." During the Vietnam War, unlike today, Guard members were not sent into battle.

"You've got to be kidding — you guys are chickens!" Steve exclaimed, scowling at them.

"Buk-buk-buk-brrr-awk!" squawked the one sitting closest to where Steve was standing.

"We ain't gonna get killed," chimed in another one.

Life at Fort Ord was easier than Fort Lewis and fairly uneventful. But it was not untouched by the disturbing effects of war. One evening just before sundown, Steve watched as a soldier who had returned from Vietnam climbed up to the top of the tallest building on the base. He began to act as if he were throwing grenades from the building at imagined Viet Cong below. Steve shuddered and worried about his own mind. *Would he survive this war with this mind intact?*

There were many soldiers who had served their one-year tour in Vietnam now at Fort Ord. Some would stumble into the barracks drunk every night, as they tried to drown out the horrors they had witnessed in the jungle in a bottle of booze. This happened night after night. The new privates watched as the drunks returned to their beds and passed out. Some threw up while they were unconscious. Steve and other men in his company would turn them over so they didn't choke on their own vomit. Steve witnessed rampant drug use for the first time in his life while at Fort Ord. He watched guys pass pills around, but he really wasn't sure what kind of pills they were. Whenever he was offered one, he just said, "No thanks." He also saw men smoking marijuana nearly everywhere around the base. Only a couple of new recruits took up smoking it with the seasoned privates, who had brought their stash back from Vietnam, where it was plentiful and easy to get.

While Steve had enlisted in the U.S. Army as a naïve preacher's son, after just a few months he had seen more of the ugly side of humanity than during his previous 18 years and he hadn't even been sent to war yet. New orders were coming in. It was time for Steve to leave California. Out of 500 new privates who were stationed at Fort Ord with Steve, all but three were sent to Vietnam. Steve was one of the three who escaped the battlefield once again.

Instead, Steve was sent to Fort Ben Harris, Indiana for what the U.S. Army called "highly specialized training." Steve was told he was going to get an administrative job. *I'll take it,* Steve thought, considering himself lucky to get an office job over the trenches of battle. He felt that somehow, God was watching out for him. For some reason, yet unknown, Steve believed God needed him to stay sane and alive. *Maybe it's thanks to Harley's prayers.* For Steve believed that God would certainly honor his dad's requests.

Steve spent four weeks training for his clerk job in Indiana before getting new orders. Once again, he dodged the bullet. This time he would go to Fort Leonard Wood in the middle of the Missouri Ozarks. He called Harley to tell him the news.

"Dad," Steve said over the line, "I've got great news. I'm not going to Nam!"

"Oh, thank God!" Harley exclaimed. Steve could hear the relief in his voice. "I can't believe that you're not being sent over there, but I'm so grateful!"

Steve hung up the phone, not quite believing his good luck either.

When Steve arrived at Fort Leonard Wood, his training was complete, and he was given a full-fledged Army job. He was handed the keys to a big, long building on the base where he would spend his days. When he reported to his office job, he saw a computer for the very first time. The giant metal box went from floor to ceiling and had blinking lights and wires coming out of it. The Army put Steve in charge of Levy Briefs, or taking care of reassignments on the base. The Levy Briefs would come down from Washington on that giant computer and would be printed on a large machine that took a spool of paper with perforated edges.

Those reports with the names on them would have the soldier's rank, Social Security number, company and the reassignment. It was Steve's job to make 50 copies of each new order and disperse them. He was shocked when the first private came into the building and asked Steve if he could help him get back to Vietnam.

"Why in the world would you want to go back to Vietnam?" Steve asked the young soldier standing at his desk. He did not even try to hide his surprise.

The freckled, redhead man — a boy really, probably all of 21 — shrugged his shoulders, and then he sighed, "I've got a kid over there, man."

"Oh," Steve said, the realization of the situation hitting him. He'd heard about American G.I.s getting their Vietnamese girlfriends pregnant.

"I'll tell you what," Steve retorted, studying the redheaded private carefully. "I have to go to the bathroom. If there's $50 on the table when I come back, I think I can help you get back to your papoose!"

Steve turned around and walked toward the restroom. When he emerged, the freckled face private was gone and a cool fifty was lying next to Steve's water glass on the desk. Steve grabbed the cash and shoved it in his pocket. Then he reached for a bottle of Whiteout and carefully covered all of the personal information on one of the reassignment papers on his desk with the name of a soldier that was supposed to go to Vietnam. In its place, he then typed in freckle-face's name and Social Security number. Then he took the sheet back to the Xerox machine and made 50 copies. He stood back and admired his work. No one would be able to tell that anything had been changed from the original order. Steve had just figured out a way to make some quick and easy cash.

Sometimes men came in and asked that someone they didn't like be shipped out to Vietnam. Steve could easily make that happen, and he'd charge $100 per request.

Much later, Steve realized the staggering magnitude that he might have sent as many as 100 men to their deaths on battlefields in Vietnam — men who were never supposed to go there. But Steve wasn't thinking about that. All he was thinking about was the cash. Even though he knew that some men probably wouldn't make it back, he really didn't care. A piece of his heart had hardened.

Others came in and asked Steve to change their orders so they didn't have to go to Nam. He didn't always have to eliminate a name from the list; sometimes he could just add them to the bottom of the page. None of his superiors ever questioned Steve's changes. In the chaos that was the Vietnam War, nobody even noticed.

One day, a private who worked an office job in the next building came running into the building where Steve worked and spurted out, "Hey Frey, I got to see the Levies on the computer before they hit your desk. You're down! You're down on Levies!"

"Oh really?" Steve said.

And sure enough, when the stack of Levies landed on Steve's desk, his name was there. In bold letters, it said, "Steve Frey." And his reassignment was for Vietnam. Steve sighed. But this time *he* was in control of his own fate. Later that night, after almost everyone on base was asleep, he grabbed his keys for the building and went back inside to his desk. No one was going to stop and question him. He often worked late into the evening. He took the bottle of Whiteout and carefully went over the words "Saigon, Vietnam." In its place he typed, "Heidelberg, Germany." Heidelberg, he had been told, was the Army's headquarters in Europe.

* * *

As Steve began processing out of Fort Leonard Wood, Missouri for Germany, he thought, *I should get married! Who I should marry?* Steve considered the letters he had exchanged with Marlene Luckey. During his last leave, he'd even driven all the way to Colorado to go on an actual date with her. When Steve arrived at her door, Marlene opened it and gave him her shy smile. It was awkward between the two of them and Marlene's overbearing mother hovered over them as they all sat down for dinner.

It was a short trip. Steve only stayed one night. Marlene's parents had been cordial to him and put him up in the guest room. Marlene was the only girl that he'd ever had any kind of relationship with. Now as he considered whom to marry, because that was what was expected of men his age, he picked up the phone and dialed Marlene's number.

"Hey, Marlene," Steve said.

"Hi, Steve," Marlene replied.

"Let's get married," Steve proclaimed.

"Sure." Marlene uttered, flatly. Something in Steve's stomach tightened, but he ignored it. He was going to have a wife to take with him when he went overseas.

In December of 1970, nearly a year to the day his draft number was drawn, Steve was granted a leave before transferring to Germany. He traveled back to Crosby, North Dakota to see his parents. Berneice and Harley greeted him with huge smiles and hugs after he stepped into the entryway of their home.

"Mom, Dad, I've got some big news!"

"What is it, son?" Harley asked.

"I'm getting married!"

"Well, good!" Harley said, congratulating him.

Berneice smiled and nodded.

"So, son, are you going to tell us *who* you're marrying?" Berneice asked.

"You remember Marlene, that girl from Hillcrest I told you about, the one I've been writing to? I went to see her in Colorado a few months ago."

"That's great, son! That's great! We can't wait to meet her," Harley declared, as he thumped Steve on the back.

Steve with Berneice & Harley when he came home to tell them he was getting married

A few days later, Harley, Berneice and Steve made the drive to Littleton, Colorado. Steve tried to feign excitement when he saw Marlene again. But he didn't feel anything. Yet he quickly shooed away any doubts that crept into his mind. He knew this was something he should do.

Marlene Luckey and Steve Frey were married on a crisp December morning inside a small white church with the picturesque Colorado Rockies in the background. There was nothing remarkable about the wedding. They had a small reception in the church basement with Steve's parents and members of Marlene's family who lived in the area. The women from the church served ham sandwiches and punch. For their honeymoon, the new Mr. and Mrs. Frey got into Steve's car and drove north to Fort Morgan, Colorado and checked into a motel. The next day they washed the car and made the long drive to West Union, Iowa, so Steve could introduce Marlene to his relatives. The marriage would last for eight years.

Chapter 6: Life in a Foreign Land

"If I speak in the tongues of men and of angels, but have not love, I am a noisy gong or a clanging cymbal. And if I have prophetic powers, and understand all mysteries and all knowledge, and if I have all faith, so as to remove mountains, but have not love, I am nothing." 1 Corinthians 13:1-2

Just days after they were married, Steve went to Heidelberg, Germany with the Army. Two months later, Marlene joined him. The young couple didn't fight, but they didn't really know either other either and each felt lonely in the marriage as well as in a foreign country. While Marlene's affection for Steve was apparent, Steve himself was unhappy. He constantly questioned himself: *Why did I marry her? I'm not in love with her! What do I do now?*

But Steve never voiced those disturbing thoughts to Marlene. He wasn't a bad husband, but he wasn't a good one either. A year and a half after arriving in Germany, Steve was eligible for an honorable discharge from the Army. Jan. 12, 1972, was his last day an enlisted man. He said to Marlene, You know, we've had a pretty nice time here in Germany."

Marlene nodded, but didn't reply.

"Well, we don't have to go home right away. There are plenty government jobs I can get here. Would you be okay with staying for a while?" he asked.

Marlene missed her parents, but she wanted to make Steve happy. Even though he had never voiced his private thoughts about their marriage, she knew somewhere, deep inside that something was wrong. But she was inexperienced and Steve was the only boy who had ever paid any attention to her. She may have known he didn't really love her, but it wasn't even something she admitted to herself.

"Whatever you want is fine, Steve," she agreed.

"Great! Then we'll stay awhile — maybe a year or so?" he looked at her, smiling. It was the first time he'd even smiled at her in months.

"Okay," she piped, a little more hopefully.

And that night Steve was more attentive to her than he had been in a long time. A few months later, Steve and Marlene went on a 10-day camping trip with friends to Interlaken, Switzerland and traveled throughout the Alps. They got along fine during that trip, but there was no real passion between them. Upon their return, Steve promised God he was going to be a better Christian and learn to love Marlene. But he still felt unsettled, even though he was married and had a job, it was as if he hadn't found his place in the world yet.

When the couple got back to Heidelberg, Steve began his civilian job registering U.S. Government vehicles in the country. Three years after arriving in Germany, Marlene gave birth to a son, whom they named Zachariah. Steve was thrilled with the birth of his son. He adored Zachariah. Steve took on the expected role of working husband and father, and Marlene stayed home with the baby and took are of the house and meals. Marlene was extremely frugal and the two were able to live quite nicely on Steve's government salary. Marlene even washed all their clothes in the bathtub and hung them out to dry rather than use the washing machine and drier, in order to save money on the couple's electric bill. Steve and Marlene never spoke a cross word to one another. Marlene was an extremely devout Christian and spent hours reading the Bible each week. Baby Zach was healthy and growing fast.

Chapter 7: Dragged Away By Desire

"But each person is tempted when they are dragged away by their own evil desire and enticed. Then, after desire has conceived, it gives birth to sin; and sin, when it is full-grown, gives birth to death." James 1: 14-15.

The year was 1974. Zach was 16 months old when Steve and Marlene decided to return to the states to be closer to family. They settled on moving to West Union, Iowa where Steve's parents, as well as a number of his relatives, were living. Upon their return, Steve decided to put his barber training to work. He opened his own barbershop on Main Street and called it *The Gentleman's Barbershop*. One of his first customers was his cousin, Al Frey, who soon became a regular.

Word soon got around town that Steve was a skilled barber, and his customer base began to grow. Even though he called it *The Gentleman's Barbershop*, women especially seemed to like the way Steve cut their hair. Soon, his clientele was about 65 percent women. Steve's Dorothy Hamill cut was the most popular among the ladies and young girls in town. Steve hired several other stylists to work in the salon and business boomed almost immediately. Steve's talents were in demand among the elite in West Union as well. Lawyers and businessmen sought out his services; one doctor even had Steve make house calls, so that he could get his haircut in the privacy of his own home. While Steve was popular among them, he felt inferior to community leaders and never saw himself as their equal.

At the same time, Steve and his dad, Harley, began to build a log home for Marlene and Zachariah and a new baby that was on the way. The log home was on a cliff, facing the Turkey River. When Steve and Harley were finished it had a fireplace and a loft. Marlene and Steve filled their home with well-constructed furniture and antiques that they had purchased while living in Germany. Jeremiah was born at the end of 1974, followed three years later by Hannah.

Marlene and Steve experienced tense moments in the delivery room when Hannah was born. The umbilical cord was wrapped around her neck and oxygen was cut off to her brain. The trauma caused Hannah to have frontal-lobe disorder, which resulted in a learning disability-and later placed her in special education classes in school. The trauma also contributed to Hannah's life-long difficulty in controlling her emotions, her ability to have empathy for others, as well as her susceptibility toward depression.

But, overall, Steve's life was going exactly how it was supposed to go. His business was doing well. His children were happy and healthy, and he had provided them a home built with his own two hands. Something was still missing for Steve, however. He couldn't quite put his finger on what it was. It was as if he was living someone else's life. Every day he felt like a fake, a phony. And on top of it, he felt worthless. Steve couldn't shake those feelings, even when all the evidence around him seemed to say otherwise. So Steve began to drink. It began insidiously, as these things do, with a little wine or beer after work. He was only 24, and he started hanging out with a couple of single men. They would drive around the small town of West Union, drinking in cars and in parks. For Steve, it was a welcome escape from the life he was expected to live.

Marlene stayed home with their young children, while he was running around town three or four nights a week. He was trying to fill the gaping hole inside of him with anything but God. Despite the drinking, he still always managed to get up the next day and go in and open the shop. Night after night, week after week, this went on, and Steve began to seek out the company of other women. There was no one special, no one he fell madly in love with, but he was always searching for someone or something better than Marlene and the cards he had been handed. Marlene's devout Christian beliefs kept her from complaining to him, even though she felt ripped apart inside.

The rumors began to fly — as they will in small communities — about Steve's gallivanting around town, being drunk and ending up in other women's beds. Marlene never said a word to him; she never questioned him at all. However, she saw women whisper to one another when she walked by a group of them in the coffee shop or grocery store. She could feel their eyes upon her, looking at her with sympathy and at Steve with disdain, every time the couple and their young children attended Sunday services. It was after one of those services that the Lutheran pastor drove out to the Freys' log cabin. The pastor knocked on the door, and Marlene opened it, with Zachariah and Jeremiah at her ankles and baby Hannah in her arms.

"Where's Steve?" Pastor Luke Johnson asked.

"He's out back," Marlene said emotionlessly. She wondered why Pastor Luke was here, but she didn't dare to question him.

Pastor Luke made his way around the side of the house to the back, where he saw Steve a few yards away by the river that ran behind the cabin. Steve had his fishing rod and was about to cast it when the Pastor Luke waved at him. Steve waved back and the pastor made his way toward him.

"Hey, Steve, can I have a minute of your time?" he asked.

"Sure thing, Pastor," Steve replied.

Steve noticed the serious look on Pastor Luke's face. He wondered what had happened. Was something going on with his mom or dad? But this wasn't about Harley or Berneice.

"Steve," Pastor Luke began, "I need to talk to you about your behavior lately."

"What?" Steve exclaimed. He began to feel flushed with embarrassment and shame.

"You know what I'm talking about, Steve. Everyone in town knows. You've been seen drunk and running around this town nearly every night for months now," Pastor Luke admonished.

Steve hung his head for a moment. He didn't know what to say.

"But, Pastor Luke," Steve said, as he tried to think of a way to defend his behavior.

"Steve," Pastor Luke said, cutting him him off, "everyone also knows about the women! You have broken your marriage vows!"

Steve couldn't believe his ears. He began to feel the hot tide of anger sweep over his body as his face turned beet red.

"Pa-Pa-Pastor Luke," Steve stuttered.

"Steve," Pastor Luke cautioned, cutting Steve off again, "I expect you to come to church next Sunday and apologize. You need to tell the entire congregation you are sorry for your behavior! Admit that you're a sinner, and then you need to ask for forgiveness!" Pastor Luke seethed with condemnation.

At that point, the red-hot anger inside of Steve came boiling over.

"How dare you judge me, Pastor Luke! It will be a cold day in hell when I stand in front of your congregation and ask for forgiveness! I want nothing to do with that kind of Christianity!"

Pastor Luke shook his head and looked at Steve with disapproval. He promptly turned and walked up the lawn toward the house. Steve watched him go and saw Marlene standing in the window with baby Hannah in her arms. Steve felt horribly ashamed. *What did I expect? Of course everyone knows. This is a small town!*

But Steve, so overwhelmed by his own shame, didn't stop to think about how his behavior was affecting Marlene. When he looked back up at the window, Marlene was no longer standing there. Steve picked up his fishing rod and cast his line into the water.

A few days later, an older woman from the church came into Steve's shop. Clara Hanson had always told Steve what a gifted speaker he was and how he should follow in his father's footsteps and become a minister.

"Steve?" Clara said, inquiringly as she approached his barber chair. The only other person in the shop that early in the morning was the receptionist, Linda, and she was on the phone booking appointments. "Steve," Clara said again. "Everyone in the congregation had so much respect for you."

Oh man, not again! Steve thought.

"Clara, if Pastor Luke sent you, I'll tell you the same thing I told him,"

"Steve," Clara said, interrupting him. "We are all worried about your family and you. Are you dealing drugs?"

"No!" Steve said, emphatically denying the suggestion. He knew he hadn't been living right, but why did everyone always expect the worst of him?

"Clara, you can leave now!" Steve instructed with a coldness in his voice that told Clara she had better do what he asked.

"Humph!" she seethed, as she whirled around and walked out the door.

The following Sunday, Marlene and the children went to church without him. Steve decided he'd call up his friend Don Landon and see if he wanted to go fishing.

"Hello?" Don answered.

"Hey, Don, it's Steve. I know you said you have a good fishing hole out on your property. How about I come out and we catch some fish?" Steve asked.

"Hold on a minute, Steve," Don said.

Don put the phone down and Steve could hear him talking with his wife in the background, but their voices were too muffled for him to make out what they were saying.

"Kathy says she wants to go out and see her folks. Come out and see us some other time," Don said, as he placed the phone back in its cradle.

Don's rejection stung. Steve listened to the dial tone for a few minutes before hanging the phone back up. *I don't have any more friends,* he thought. *No one in this town wants anything to do with me.*

A few days later, Steve knocked on Harley's door. Harley answered it and ushered Steve inside. "Dad, I have failed. I've failed at marriage. I've broken my marriage vows, and I have been with other women. I've failed at everything in my life," Steve told Harley with his voice shaking.

Harley looked long and hard at his son; his blue eyes seemed to pierce Steve's soul. Then he took a deep breath and spoke. "There's only one way out, Steve — you have to face the truth. You go tell Marlene and ask for her forgiveness," Harley admonished, matter-of-factly.

That night, after the children were in bed, Steve asked Marlene to sit down at the kitchen table. Steve sighed and began: "I've failed, Marlene. I've failed in my marriage and keeping my vows to you. There have been other women — nobody special, nobody whom I'm in love with. I just have failed you and the kids," Steve said as tears began running down his face.

Marlene's flinch was barely detectable. She had known, of course — talk had spread like wildfire around the little town of West Union. But it was less painful for her to pretend to not know the truth about what her husband was doing. She let out a long sigh and then stood up and came around the table toward Steve. Marlene then put her hand on his shoulder and looked him in the eye and said unwavering, "Steve, I forgive you."

Steve couldn't believe how calm Marlene was. He expected her to get angry, and a part of him secretly hoped she'd throw him out. He wanted out of this loveless marriage, but he wasn't brave enough just to say so. He just couldn't handle the guilt of leaving yet.

Steve gulped. He gained a new respect for Marlene in that moment. He hadn't realized how strong of a woman she really was — and it hit him with a jolt that he had never given her enough credit.

Despite that, as the days passed, Steve continued to feel his life spiral out of control. He wanted to run for cover to avoid all the condemning eyes he encountered everywhere he went in West Union. One night after he left the shop, he poured himself a beer, and as he drank it he made a decision. He wanted out. He would sell *The Gentlemen's Barbershop.*

Steve didn't have a plan or think it through very well, but when he told a couple of women stylists he had hired about his desire to sell the place, they told him *they* would buy the business. Within two weeks, Steve was no longer the owner of the shop on Main Street, and he quit cutting hair altogether.

A week or two went by. Steve had just been moping around at home. Marlene had voiced her concerns about what was happening with Steve to his family, and Berneice came up with a plan and enlisted her brother's wife, Delores', help. The two women drove up to the log home one morning and knocked on the door. Steve answered and was surprised to see his mother and her sister-in-law standing before him.

"What do you need, mom?" Steve asked.

"Can we come in?" Berneice said, looking at him with concern.

"Okay, sure," Steve said, agreeably.

The two women stepped into the entryway.

"Steve," Berneice said, "we'd like you to come on a ride with us."

"A ride?" Steve asked in a puzzled way. "Where are we going?"

Berneice paused for a moment, "Nowhere, Steve. Delores and I just want to talk to you, right Delores?" Berneice said, glancing over at Delores. Delores, who wanted to appease her sister-in-law, nodded her head in agreement.

"Okay, I guess," Steve said, reluctantly.

The three of them walked toward Berneice's brown Buick. Steve got into the backseat, while Delores got in front with his mother. His mother put the car into gear and began to drive.

"What do you want to talk about?" Steve asked, still trying to figure out what was going on.

"Steve, it's all over town. Everyone is talking about your drinking and taking up with other women. And now you've gone and quit your business! We're just worried about you," Berneice lamented.

"You don't have to worry about me, Mom!" Steve said, resentfully. But he could also feel the hot flash of shame spread over him. *Now, even my mother has turned against me*, he thought.

"Hey," he said, looking around as his mom turned onto Highway 63, heading north. "Where are we going?"

"We just want to help you Steve," Delores chimed in.

"What? How? Where are you taking me? Mom? Delores?" Steve began to panic.

"Settle down, Steve!" Berneice scolded. "We just made an appointment for you with a doctor in Minneapolis. Just give him a chance. We really think he can help you?"

"With what, Mom? I don't need a doctor? This is crazy."

"Well, we think you do, don't we, Delores?" Berneice admonished, giving Delores, who was sitting in the passenger seat, a knowing glance. Bernice steered the car north on the highway as Delores nodded in agreement.

Steve slumped back in the seat. *His own mother and her sister-in-law were holding him hostage! This is ridiculous*, he thought.

During the remainder of the three-hour drive to Minneapolis, the three sat in silence. Berneice made an attempt at some small talk, mentioning something about the weather or the neighbors, but her efforts to get Steve to chime in were in vain. Finally, after what seemed like forever to Steve, his mother pulled the car in front of a psychiatric hospital near downtown Minneapolis. She let Steve and Delores out.

"I'm going to park the car, Steve. Delores, you let them know Steve is here for his appointment with Dr. Richardson."

"Okay, Berneice," Delores said. And when Steve didn't respond, Berneice pointed outward,

"Steve, all you have to do is talk to Dr. Richardson. That's all I'm asking you to do."

Begrudgingly Steve turned and followed Delores inside the pristine white clinic. Delores went up to the desk and gave the receptionist Steve's name. Steve slumped into a waiting room seat. The chairs were hard and had metal handles. The white, cement blocks walls seemed to mock him. He glared at his mother when she came in after parking the car and sat down beside him. The two did not speak.

When the nurse called Steve's name, he followed her back to the doctor's office. The psychiatrist, Dr. Matthew Richardson, was an older man with jet-black hair and gray eyes. He donned spectacles that sat on the bridge of his nose. He was sitting in a leather chair behind a massive oak desk. He motioned for Steve to take a seat across from him.

"Hello, Steve. I'm Dr. Richardson. Take a seat. I spoke to your mother last week, and I'd like to ask *you*, Steve, why are *you* here?"

"Because my mom told me I had to see you. She didn't give me a choice!" Steve said, seething.

"What's bothering you, Steve?"

"Nothing — nothing is bothering me!" Steve said defensively. "Just leave me alone."

Dr. Richardson went on to ask Steve a number of questions, which Steve answered with a terse "yes" or "no." Finally, Dr. Richardson cleared his throat and pushed his chair back away from his desk.

"Excuse me a moment." Dr. Richardson said. Then he got up and left the room, closing the door behind him. Steve sat and stared at the psychiatric diplomas on the wall for what seemed like an eternity. But in actuality, it was about 30 minutes later that the doctor returned with Berneice.

"Steve, I've spoken with your mother. Now you go home and relax."

Steve was perplexed. *Go home and relax? Why in the world did we drive all the way here?*

Steve shrugged his shoulders and followed Berneice out of the room and into the lobby, where Berneice motioned to Delores to join them. The three walked out the clinic's door and into the parking lot. Once they got back into the car Steve asked, "Mom, what in the world was that all about?"

"We are worried about you, Steve. We just wanted to see what the doctor would say," she insisted.

"What did he say to you, Mom?" Steve asked. "I know he said something. I was sitting in his office by myself for a long time."

"Just that you're suffering from anxiety, Steve. We're supposed to treat you with kid gloves. He says you're on the verge of a nervous breakdown," Berneice fretted, glancing at him in the rearview mirror.

Steve shook his head. He felt a million times worse than he did after the preacher confronted him, and that was humiliating enough.

"What a waste, Mom," Steve grumbled, shaking his head.

The rest of the long ride home, Delores and Berneice talked to one another while Steve sulked in the backseat.

Chapter 8: The Final Straw

"For the Lord will not cast off forever, but, though he cause grief, he will have compassion according to the abundance of his steadfast love; for he does not willingly afflict or grieve the children of men." Lamentations 3:31-33

While Steve had sold his business, with three young children at home he still needed to earn a living. He called his friend, Jim Larsen, who was a farmer, and said, "Hey Jim, I should come work for you. You need any help out there on your farm?"

"As a matter of fact, Steve, I do! I can't pay you much, but I'll pay what I can," Jim told him, enthusiastically.

"Okay, great! How about tomorrow?" Steve asked.

"Sounds good. Why don't you get out here at about seven tomorrow morning."

Jim Larsen had about 80 acres of land where he grew corn and beans. He also raised several hundred chickens. Steve helped Jim milk cows and scoop manure in the chicken coop into a spreader to fertilize the crops. After a few weeks of that kind of work, the chicken manure had eaten away at Steve's boots because it was so high in ammonia. It was dirty, smelly work, but Steve didn't mind. It seemed fitting to him that he was up to his ankles in manure after the mess he had made of his life. Jim didn't pay him much — just what he could spare here and there.

Jim Larsen had three girls that always seemed to be around when Jim and Steve were working. The oldest two daughters, 11-year-old Abigail and nine-year-old Emily, were able to help with many of the chores. The baby, Melinda, who was six-years-old, usually played nearby. All three girls were toeheads, and their blonde locks bobbed in the bright sunshine of the late July days. Melinda's golden curls fell around her face and her cherub cheeks were red from the heat and sun. Melinda was the precious baby who was the apple of her father's eye. Jim would hoist Melinda up on his shoulders, and Steve and the other two girls would make their way around the farm, singing and laughing as they went from chore to chore. Steve spent more time with Jim's children than he did his own. But every time he looked into the eyes of his own children, his sense of failure increased and he couldn't handle the waves of guilt that swept over him.

One of those hot July days, Steve, Jim and the girls were out in the field working. That day, Jim was driving the tractor that pulled the manure spreader along the crops. They had stopped for a moment for a water break, and Jim jumped down from the tractor to join the others. The girls often took turns riding on the tractor with Jim, as the others followed alongside to make sure the manure was spread out evenly. After taking a swig of water and wiping the sweat from his brow with his handkerchief, Jim climbed back up on the tractor and started to put it in gear. He didn't realize that little Melinda had jumped onto the back of the tractor, intending to ride along with him.

Jim let the clutch out and jolt caused Melinda to lose her grip on the machine and she fell right under the wheel. Jim, suddenly realizing that Melinda wasn't on the back of the tractor anymore, slammed on the breaks. But it was too late; the unimaginable had happened. The tractor's giant wheel had rolled over Melinda's head and crushed it.

Steve watched the scene unfold in shock, unable to act quickly enough to do anything to stop it. He looked at the ground and saw Melinda's crushed skull. Jim jumped down from the tractor and saw his baby girl on the ground with blood soaking her blond curls. Jim began to scream hysterically and wave his hands above his head. He ran for the neighbor's farm, bellowing, "Help! Help!"

Steve bolted for the other two girls, who were on the other side of the tractor and had not witnessed the horrific accident. Steve grabbed both girls by the arms,

"Get in the car," he ordered frantically, as he ushered them toward the old blue Ford pickup that was parked a few yards away. "Now!" Steve shouted.

The girls could hear the panic in his voice and did as they were ordered. Steve sped with the girls toward the Larsens' farmhouse, about eight miles away. Nancy, Jim's wife, was inside making the large noon meal, which was customary for farmwives to do while the men worked in the fields. Steve brought the car to a screeching halt right outside the door to the house and leaped out, while the other two girls gripped one another, paralyzed by fear in the back of the pickup.

"Nancy! Nancy! I need you!" Steve yelled.

Nancy came to the door. As she opened it, she looked at him quizzically, "What is it, Steve? What's wrong?"

"I don't know where Jim is," Steve shrieked. "There's been an accident, out in the field. It's Melinda — she's dead, Nancy! She's dead!"

Nancy's legs buckled out from under her and she fell to her knees. Her mother, who had been helping her prepare the meal, appeared at the door and rushed to Nancy's side. She helped her up and back into the house, and motioned for the two girls to follow her. Sobbing, Abigail and Emily held onto each other as they made their way into the house behind their mother and grandmother.

Steve stood there, not knowing what to do next. But he didn't want to be there when Jim returned. He was overwhelmed with panic. *I've got to get out of here,* he thought. He quickly walked toward his old Pontiac parked near the barn, got in and drove off.

Chapter 9: Fall from Grace

"Now the Spirit speaketh expressly, that in the latter times some shall depart from the faith, giving heed to seducing spirits, and doctrines of devils." I Timothy 4:1

A silence fell over the town of West Union in the days that followed Melinda's death and led up to her funeral. When someone dies in a farm accident in a small community, it affects everyone. But when the death is of a child, the pain is magnified. The news spread through town in hushed whispers from neighbor to neighbor. Steve locked himself in his and Marlene's bedroom and refused to come out, even as Marlene pounded on the door and begged him to eat something or at least take a shower.

On the Friday morning that Melinda's funeral was held, the townspeople, dressed in shades of gray and black, packed the small Lutheran church. Many were forced to stand out on the steps because there was no room inside the sanctuary. Steve had gotten out of bed and put on his only black suit for the occasion. He arrived at the church just a few minutes before the service was to start. Marlene, not thinking it was appropriate for the children to attend, had taken them over to a cousin's house. Marlene had arrived well before Steve.

As Steve approached the church, everyone turned to stare at him as he climbed the steps. He felt reproach in their eyes. Steve looked straight ahead, not daring to make eye contact with anyone. But he knew what they were thinking: *There he is, that scumbag! I bet this is his fault. Why did the Larsens even have that loser around their kids anyway?*

Plagued with those thoughts, Steve made his way to the front of the church and took a seat in a pew right behind the Larsen family. Steve hung his head as the pallbearers carrying the small, white coffin slowly brought it toward the altar. Sobbing could be heard throughout the crowd. Steve stole a glance toward Nancy, who looked ashen, with tears streaming down her face. Jim, by her side, showed no expression at all; he just stared blankly ahead.

Everything I'm involved in goes bad, Steve thought. *I am a curse to everyone I meet. Everything I touch is rotten.* It was like a broken record playing over and over again in Steve's mind. To him, this was the end of his life in West Union. He could no longer face these people or what he had done ever again.

* * *

As the sun rose on the hot July day following Melinda's funeral, Steve awoke. His head was pounding. He tried to remember the events of the day before. Gradually, the fuzziness in his brain from the alcohol he had consumed the night before began to clear. And then it hit him: *The little girl was dead. Melinda was gone. And he had witnessed the whole thing happen and he couldn't stop it. Everyone was blaming him!* The truth hit him smack in the face like a cold, wet towel.

He was alone in his and Marlene's marital bed. The shades were drawn shut and the room was dark. He knew that everyone would be better off if he were gone. *If I weren't such a chicken* — he chided himself — *I'd put an end to it now and just kill myself!* But what his father, the preacher, had told him about what happened to people who commit suicide had scared him at a very young age. Images of an eternity of pain even worse that what he was feeling now — along with fire and brimstone — filled his head. He felt so small. But then another idea began to form in his mind. He would leave! He would run away! Everyone would be happier without him. He had no plan, no idea where he would go. He would just go. Then his wife, his children, his parents and this whole damn town could breathe a sigh of relief. Real tears of self-pity streamed down his face. His father's judgmental eyes kept looming in his mind. He could probably deal with letting everyone else down, but not him. A lifetime of feeling as if he had always disappointed his dad would culminate in the next few moments as he decided what he would do next.

Steve pushed himself out of the bed, his head pounding. He made his way over to the small desk in the bedroom and pulled out a piece of paper and a pen. He fumbled through a couple of more drawers, before finding a few bills Marlene had tucked away. He took a fifty and set it on the desk next to the paper and pen. Then as he lowered himself into the desk chair, he picked up the pen and began to write:

> Dad,
> *I love you, but I don't need you preaching at me. You've done nothing but preach at me my whole life. I'm leaving. Do not come looking for me, until you can just say, "I love you." That's all I want, is just to have you love me, no matter what happens. I will let you know where I am, when you can do that.*
> *Love,*
> *Steve*

Steve took an envelope out of another drawer, put the letter inside and sealed it. Then he got up, grabbed the letter and the $50. He hastily threw a few clothes into a duffle bag and walked into the living room.

Zachariah, Jeremiah and Hannah were gathered about the TV watching Saturday morning cartoons, and Marlene was making them breakfast in the kitchen. Steve motioned for Marlene to follow him to the front of the house and then he went outside on the front step; Marlene followed.

"Marlene, I'm leaving. I have taken fifty dollars out of the desk. That's all I will take. You can have everything else. I want you to give this letter to my dad, please." Steve pleaded, handing her the letter.

Marlene couldn't bear to look at him, so she looked down at the ground. There were so many things she wanted to say, could have said — but instead she just squeaked out a soft, *"okay."*

Just then Zachariah, Jeremiah and Hannah came rushing to the door, pressing their noses against the screen. "Mommy, we're hungry, when is breakfast?" Jeremiah asked.

"In a minute, kids," Marlene spluttered, her voice trembling.

"Daddy, what are you doing? Are ya' goin' someplace?" Zachariah asked.

"Yes, Zach," Steve said. "Daddy has to go away for a while."

"Where to, Daddy? Why do you have to go? Can you take me with you?" Zachariah pleaded.

Steve looked down at his three children and couldn't take their sweet little faces looking at him this way, trying to understand what was going on — especially little Hannah, who looked as if she were about to cry. Steve averted his eyes from theirs.

"Don't worry, kids," Steve said, trying to reassure them. "Daddy will see you soon."

But Steve knew it was a lie. He bent down to give each child a kiss and struggled to hold back his tears. Then he stood up and looked at Marlene, who continued to stare at the ground.

"Bye now, kids," he said. And with that, Steve raised his hand to wave at them as he walked toward his Pontiac parked next to the garage. He stopped in the garage and grabbed a tent and an electric skillet and threw them into his trunk.

"I'll let you know where I'm at, Marlene," Steve promised as he opened the door of the car and climbed inside. She didn't respond.

Steve had no idea where he was going, as he pulled out of the long driveway and onto the dirt road. He looked in the rearview mirror at the house he had built with his own two hands for his family. But soon, the dust from the gravel made it impossible to see his home anymore.

Chapter 10: The Lost Years
"Some wandered in desert wastelands finding no way to a city where they could settle. They were hungry and thirsty, and their lives ebbed away." Psalm 107: 4-5

Steve pointed the car toward Waterloo. As he approached the town where he had spent a year of his life attending Barber College, he realized he didn't want to come back to this place where he had lived in fear during the race riots. As he drove by the school where he learned to cut hair, he wondered why in the world he had gone there. *Why had he picked that profession?* He began to question every decision he had ever made — most of all, why had he married Marlene? He passed through Waterloo and headed west.

After another couple of hours, he reached the outskirts Des Moines. It was getting late. He remembered he had a friend who lived in Iowa's capital city whom he'd met in Waterloo while he was in barber school. Jim Ahrens had been working in Waterloo for an ophthalmologist at the time and had rented a room in the same boarding house where Steve lived. Steve remembered that the last time he'd run into him, Jim had told him where he and his wife had moved to in Des Moines. He hoped that Jim still lived there.

It was getting dark as Steve drove through the less-desirable area of Des Moines' northwest side, near the Firestone Tire & Rubber Company. The smell from the tire factory permeated the air. Steve pulled up to Jim and Georgie Ahrens' dilapidated home. Jim and Georgie had one 14-year-old son named Wayne. The tiny, two-bedroom house was cramped already, but when Steve knocked on the door, Jim invited him in.

"This is a surprise!" Jim proclaimed, sounding genuinely glad to see him. Jim was just a year older than Steve, but he was already balding. He wore dark-rimmed glasses and had a large spare tire around his waist.

"What are you doing here, Steve?"

"Can you help an old friend out?" Steve asked. "I need a place to stay."

"Of course, no problem, friend." Jim said, looking at Steve quizzically. He didn't ask Steve what he was doing in Des Moines. But he thought that Steve looked rough, not at all like the young man he knew in Waterloo.

Jim led Steve to Wayne's narrow bedroom. Wayne slept on a cot on one side of the room.

"We'll put another cot on the other side here," Jim said, pointing to the wall just three feet away from Wayne's bed.

"I really appreciate it, Jim," Steve said.

Jim left Steve standing in that narrow room while he went to get the cot out of the hall closet. Just then, Wayne came into his room and introduced himself to Steve. Wayne had a big, black lab at his heels.

"This is JoJo," Wayne told Steve, referring to the animal.

It was getting late by the time Jim put up the cot. Jim offered Steve a beer, and the two men sat in the living room and drank while Georgie stood looking out the kitchen window, smoking a cigarette. Georgie was an obese woman who wore a dirty, printed smock and black polyester pants. Her brown, greasy hair framed her chubby face. Steve thanked Jim for his hospitality and told him he was exhausted and he wanted to turn in. Steve collapsed on the cot, falling asleep almost immediately. It wasn't a comfortable bed, but that night Steve took no notice.

Steve awoke to JoJo's barking the next morning. At first he couldn't remember where he was. But then it all came flooding back to him: Melinda's death, taking the $50 and leaving his wife and children and somehow ending up here at Jim Ahrens' house in Des Moines. Steve threw back the blanket and swung his legs around to get up from the cot, only to step right into a mountain of dog poop, left by JoJo.

"Crap!" Steve exclaimed, followed by a few expletives. Steve hopped on one foot toward the bathroom to clean off the dog feces. By the light of day, Steve saw how filthy the Ahrens' home was. As he made his way into the bathroom, he thought it looked like no one had *ever* cleaned it. He grabbed for a grimy towel and wiped off his foot. Then he stuck it in the bathtub and begun running water over it. The smell was almost more than Steve could take. But the irony didn't escape him. His whole life had ended up being a pile of crap and here he was stepping right in it.

After drying off his foot with another grimy towel, Steve made his way into the kitchen, where Georgie was sitting with a cup of coffee. He saw a cockroach scurry across the linoleum floor. Steve felt like gagging, but instead offered Georgie a weak smile.

"There's coffee over there." She motioned toward the Mr. Coffee machine. "Help yourself!" Georgie smiled, revealing several missing teeth.

Steve thanked her and looked around for a clean mug. But the dirty dishes piled up around the sink didn't look promising.

"You'll have to clean out a cup for yourself," Georgie scowled. "I ain't no maid."

Steve found a mug and rinsed it out in the filthy sink. *No,* he thought, *she certainly isn't a maid.* But he didn't want to appear rude; after all, the Ahrens had given him a place to sleep and hadn't even questioned him about why he was there.

"Jim's already at work, over at the tire factory," Georgie told him, even though he hadn't asked. "He works the early morning shift. You can usually find him at Joe's Bar, over next to the factory, by noon. How long you gonna be here?" she questioned.

"I don't know," Steve said. And he didn't. He had no plans. He just knew he couldn't go back to West Union.

Steve spent a few nights at the Ahrens' house. He spent his days driving around Des Moines or just sitting in his car. When

Jim got off work, Steve would meet him at the bar and the two would drink until suppertime. Jim didn't seem to mind Steve staying there, even if Georgie did. And Wayne never said a word about it, although his loud snoring woke Steve many times during the night. But occasionally Jim would tell Steve he couldn't stay on a particular night — sometimes Jim and Georgie had family in town or friends were coming over. On those nights, Steve would either sleep in his car or pitch a tent in a nearby park. Sometimes he drove over to the small town of Colfax, because he knew the local police wouldn't kick him out of the park there.

In the meantime, Steve decided he'd better get some kind of job to feed himself. A man he'd met through Jim, in Joe's Bar, had told him there was an opportunity with a sporting goods company. They needed a salesman to go from school to school, selling windbreakers with the school's mascot on it. Steve drove his Pontiac from one school to the next, asking for the principal. Most of the time, he was turned away, without ever getting into the administrator's office. Occasionally, someone would take pity on him and listen to his sales pitch. But they never wanted to buy any of the cheaply made, overpriced jackets.

Nearly every night after supper, Jim and Steve would head over to *Big Earl's Goldmine,* a strip club in the warehouse district on the north side. At night, the only people in the area were bar patrons. The parking lot was littered with crushed beer cans, empty liquor bottles and used condoms. Occasionally a used syringe was in the mess. Across the street was another strip club called *Proud Mary's*, which was even more rundown and shabby than *Big Earl's.* Flashing neon, pink lights outside of each establishment advertised, "Topless Girls," and "Nude Dancers XXX."

Steve and Jim made their way past a big, black bouncer sitting in the entrance of *Big Earl's.* Security was tighter than usual that night because there had just been a stabbing at the strip joint the previous night. Neon beer signs hung on the wall and next to some of them were nude pictures of exotic dancers, often autographed by the women. Black lights were positioned above the stage and a low railing wrapped around the stage to put some distance between the dancers and the men who sat at the tables lining the raised platform. There were mirrors on the walls and behind the bar. While it was dark inside, you could sit almost anywhere and see a nude woman dancing on the stage by looking at the mirrors.

Jim would get much drunker than Steve on these nights, but Steve was always inebriated too. One evening during one of their regular trips to *Big Earl's*, there were a dozen motorcycles parked out front. Members of Hells Angels were inside. The bikers were a frightening bunch, with mostly long hair, beards and tattoos. They wore leather and denim, and they riled the strippers dancing on the stage, often grabbing for the women's breasts, which wasn't allowed. The women could grind their bodies against the men, but the men were not supposed to touch them. On this particular night, one of the bikers grabbed a dancer who had just been gyrating at Jim's and Steve's table. She sat on Steve's lap, while he became aroused.

When she made her way over the bikers' table, the guy sitting in the closest chair to Steve grabbed her. Steve stood up.

"You gonna do something about this, buddy?" the grimy biker snarled.

"You bet I am you f#$%&r!" Steve exclaimed in a drunken state and lunged toward the man. Then everything went black. When Steve came to, he was lying on the sticky, beer-soaked floor of the bar. He looked around. The bikers were gone. Jim had sunk to the floor next to him and was leaning against the wall.

"Welcome baaaack," Jim slurred. "You're damn lucky that dude didn't knife you, ya know. He just sucker-punched you, right between the eyes, and you were out cold, buddy!"

Yeah, Steve thought, *damn lucky*. He had no doubt that if he'd been killed he would have gone right to hell, considering the life he'd been living. He held his head in his hands. The pain was excruciating.

"C-c-cmon," Jim sputtered. "We gotta get outta here."

Jim pulled Steve to his feet, and the two men stumbled out of Big Earl's.

Another time, Steve found himself lying in the parking lot outside of *Proud Mary's*, just coming to after getting sucker-punched by a different biker. He couldn't even remember what the fight was about — probably over some woman. He looked around for Jim, but he was long gone. Steve somehow dragged himself to his car. The next thing he remembered was waking up, slumped over the wheel in a parking lot in Ankeny, which is about 30 miles north of Des Moines. He wasn't sure how he even got there, but he must have driven. He started up the Pontiac and drove over to a gas station to fill up the vehicle before he returned to Jim's house.

For months, the two men went on with the same routine, drinking at Joe's from noon to 4 p.m., and then hitting the strip joints after supper. Steve would often hook up with a waitress or stripper on these nights, after their shift was over. They would have sex in his car or in the back of the club. Steve felt dirty. He knew it was wrong. *But at this point*, he rationalized, *what did it matter?* Jim had his own infidelities. Often, after they would return to Jim's and Georgie's house late at night, Steve could hear the couple, fighting drunkenly, in the next room.

One morning, Steve got up earlier than usual to drive to Carroll, Iowa. His head was pounding. He downed a couple of Alka-Seltzers and poured himself a cup of strong coffee. He had a meeting with a school principal in Carroll, about an hour and a half away, to give him a sales pitch on the jackets he was selling. He jumped in his Pontiac and was just outside of Perry, on Highway 141, when he began to smell something. He pulled the car over onto the shoulder, and smoke began bellowing out from underneath the hood.

Steve yanked the door of the car open and ran toward the hood. When he opened it, the engine burst into flames. He bolted for the passenger side of the car and grabbed a couple of dirty blankets from the backseat. He had the blankets in his car from the nights he slept in the backseat. With both blankets in hand, he ran to the front of the car and threw them on the flaming engine and then threw himself on top of them. He managed to smother out the fire.

Then Steve lowered himself onto the gravel of the shoulder and leaned against the left rear tire of the car and began to cry. Other cars went speeding by him as he sobbed and sobbed.

"God, why are letting this happen to me? Haven't I suffered enough? Now my car, too?" Steve screamed out loud.

"Why, God, why? Can't anything go right in my life? Why are you letting all this torment into my life? Can't I even win at anything? I've gone from having a nice home and now I don't even have a car. It's gone downhill fast, man!" Steve shouted into traffic passing in front of him.

Steve went back and forth over the next 10 minutes — cursing at God for his trouble to begging for help. Then he got up, opened the car door and sat back down in the driver's seat. He hesitated for a moment and then softly pleaded, "Please, God, help me."

He put the key in the ignition and turned it. Miraculously the engine started up immediately. *Maybe God is listening*, Steve thought.

He drove the rest of the way to Carroll and even made it to his appointment on time with the school principal, who failed to buy a single jacket. Immediately following the rejection, Steve pulled into a convenience store just outside of town and bought a 12-pack of beer. He threw the beer onto the passenger seat next to him and cracked one open. He drove the 93 miles back to Des Moines, downing beer after beer. He also forgot all about the miracle of his car starting up again after it was on fire.

* * *

Months passed. Occasionally Steve would drive back to West Union to see his three children. He did love those kids and he missed them. He carried their pictures in his wallet and would often sit in his car, looking at their innocent faces and cry. This was back in the days before mobile phones. He never gave Marlene any warning — he would just show up.

"Daddy, Daddy, you're home!" Zachariah exclaimed from inside the entryway of the house as he saw Steve approaching. Zachariah was so excited to see his father that he stretched his hand out and pushed on the screen door, only to have his hand go right through a glass pane. Blood began to ooze from Zachariah's wrist. Steve ran toward the door and grabbed him, putting pressure on the nasty cut.

"Marlene," Steve shouted. "Come quickly. We've got to get him to the hospital. Now!"

Steve and Marlene drove their little boy to the emergency room, where the doctor stitched up the deep cut on his wrist. Maybe it was their bond over their children, or Steve's desperate attempt to do something right, but Marlene wanted to reconcile. That night Marlene and Steve shared their bed again. But it didn't last.

By the cold light of day, Steve knew his feelings for Marlene were not love. He felt worse than ever about himself the following morning, as he looked over at Marlene, who was asleep next to him. He had a sinking feeling in the pit of his stomach. He gingerly got out of bed and quietly put on his clothes and crept toward the door, closing it gently behind him. He popped his head into his children's room and looked at their angelic faces, peacefully asleep. He glanced at Zachariah's wrist, which was bandaged up.

"I love you," Steve whispered to all three of them as Jeremiah stirred in bed. Steve slowly backed away from the door and walked down the hall and out the front door. He jumped into his old Pontiac and started it up, and he drove away.

A few weeks later Marlene filed for divorce. Steve told her he didn't want anything — that she could have the house and all its contents as well as their children. Seven months after their divorce was finalized, Marlene gave birth to a baby girl, conceived on that night Steve and Marlene spent together after Zachariah's accident. Marlene named her Dinah. While Steve came back to West Union to see Dinah in the hospital, he did not have much time with her. A few weeks after she was born,

Marlene packed up their four children and moved them back home to be close to her parents in Denver.

Chapter 11: Rock Bottom

And the Lord turned and looked at Peter. And Peter remembered the saying of the Lord, how he had said to him, 'Before the rooster crows today, you will deny me three times.' And he went out and wept bitterly." Luke 22:61

Steve had worn out his welcome with Jim and Georgie in Des Moines. He had to find someplace else to live. Pitching a tent in a park or sleeping in the backseat of the Pontiac just wasn't working for him anymore. He was getting sick of himself and feeling like a freeloader. He was brought up to work hard, and there was still a part of him that felt compelled to do that.

He'd heard about a barbershop that was hiring in Monticello, Iowa, which was 167 miles northeast of Des Moines. The shop was called *Rod's Styling Barn* and was owned by Rod Kotenbrink. The building was red and in the shape of a barn. Rod gave Steve the job, so Steve rented a room in a rundown boarding house for $20 a week, just a few blocks over from downtown.

Steve wasn't making much money as a barber, so he also got a job waiting tables a few nights a week from 6 p.m. until midnight at a truck stop, where two state highways intersected in Monticello. Months passed and Steve wasn't getting any further ahead. He couldn't make ends meet, even though he was working two jobs. He was still drinking a lot. He was also having casual sex with women at the truck stop. But he had no real friends, and he had all but lost touch with his family.

And then one day, out of the blue, Harley, his dad, showed up at *Rod's Styling Barn.* Steve was in the middle of cutting a young man's hair when he glanced over at the doorway. A bell on top jingled as Harley walked through the door. Harley stood in the entryway, looking around until he spotted Steve at his booth. Steve held up his finger, indicating to Harley to wait a minute and finished the haircut he was giving. He walked toward the register with the customer, who paid his bill and left.

Then Steve turned to Harley and asked, "What are you doing here, Dad?"

"Steve, we need to talk," Harley demanded, frowning. "Can we go outside?"

"Sure," Steve shrugged. Harley seemed angry. A pit of self-pity and anxiety began forming in Steve's stomach. Shame overcame him, like a cloud casting a shadow on the ground.

The father and son stepped outside the shop and began walking down the sidewalk. It was mid-October and the leaves had started to change color. While it was an idyllic fall day — the kind that Midwesterners love to talk about — there was nothing peaceful about their conversation.

"You need to get your act together, son. You've got responsibilities — children who need you! What in God's name are doing here in Monticello?"

"Dad, didn't you read my letter? I told you," Steve paused mid-sentence as his voice shook with emotion. "Don't come and talk to me unless you can tell me you love me! Is that why you're here? It sure doesn't seem like it!"

"Steve, you need to grow up. Be a man! Stop running away from your problems," Harley admonished.

"I don't need you to scold me, Dad. Just go back home and leave me alone!" Steve demanded, his voice rising.

And with that Harley did an about-face and stormed toward his car. He did not look back as he opened the door, got in and drove away.

And that was the final straw in Steve's mind, as the Thanksgiving of 1979 approached. The holiday intensified Steve's feelings of loneliness and inadequacy. He couldn't shake the dark gray clouds that invaded his brain as he walked home from his shift at the truck stop that Thanksgiving Day. That was the day he planned to kill himself, alone in his room in the sleazy boarding house. The day he picked up his rifle with shaking hands, trying to decide whether to point it at his chest or his head.

But after loading his rifle and ultimately deciding to put the barrel in his mouth, another thought popped into Steve's mind. It was an idea that was ingrained in him as a child: the image of burning in Hades, with the Devil taunting him. *If I pull this trigger, I'm going to Hell!*

While Steve had felt uncertain about nearly everything in his life up to this point, that was the one thing he was certain of now. An eternity in a worse place with more pain than what he was feeling now awaited him if he killed himself. He began to sob silently, his chest heaving, but with no tears falling from his eyes. He laid back onto the bed, the rifle at his side. His sobs subsided, and he fell into a restless sleep.

Steve woke up the next morning and went to work, as usual. But he couldn't shake the depression that had seized him. A week passed uneventfully and then Steve got another visitor. It was his uncle, Glen, with whom he shared a middle name. Just like Harley had, Glen found Steve cutting hair in Monticello. This time, Steve was about to begin cutting a customer's hair when Glen walked into the shop. He waved at Steve and smiled. Steve excused himself from the customer in the chair and walked toward his Uncle Glen.

"What are you doing here, Glen?"

"Hey, Steve, I see you're busy. Can you take a break?" Glen asked.

Steve told him he could, after he finished the current haircut, and agreed to meet Glen at a diner a block away. A half-hour later, Steve walked over to the restaurant and sat down at a booth across from Glen.

"I'm worried about you, Steve," Glen began. "I just came to see if there was anything I could do to help. What do you need?" Glen asked, without any sound of judgment in his voice.

"I don't know," Steve shook his head. "I need a better job. I need more money so I can support my kids."

"Okay," Glen softened. "Let me see what I can do."

Just then the waitress came by with a Coke and sat it down in front of Glen.

"What can I get you?" she asked Steve.

"I'll take a Coke, too," he told her. As she left, Glen began to speak again.

"Steve, I know you can do better. I know what a hard worker you are. You've just been down on your luck. But I believe that things will turn around for you."

Glen reached down into his pocket and pulled out a $50 bill. Then he pushed it across the table toward Steve.

"Here," he insisted, "Take this." Before Steve could object, he added, "No arguments, Steve, take it."

Steve did as he was told and pushed the bill into his pocket. The two men talked about their mutual relatives and what was happening back in West Union for a little while. Then Steve got up and thanked Glen for his visit and told him he had to get back to work. He had another customer coming in soon.

"Thank you, Uncle Glen."

It wasn't so much what Glen had said, but *how* he had said it that had made an impression on Steve. *Someone still cared; someone who wasn't here to judge him or make him feel ashamed about his decisions.*

A short time later, Steve got a message while he was working at *Rod's Styling Barn.* It was from Al Frey, the cousin whose hair he cut back in West Union. There was a number for Steve to return the call.

"Steve, I'm glad you called me back!" Al said after Steve placed the call.

"I've been looking for you. Uncle Glen told me where you were," Al said.

"Okay," Steve said, hesitatingly. He wondered why this cousin, whom he hadn't seen in years, would suddenly be looking for him.

"Steve, you built that log house, and I've been thinking about that. I know you're a hard worker. How would you like to start over in life?"

"I'd like that," Steve proclaimed, his voice shaking. "What do you have in mind?"

"Up in the small town of Chester, Iowa, there's a pallet manufacturer. It's a big place. SMI — Seedorff Masonry Industries — out of Strawberry Point, Iowa owns it. That's my company. I'm vice president. We're looking for an assistant manager at the facility in Chester. I'd like to give you a chance," Al told him.

"Really?" Steve said incredulously. He couldn't believe that someone actually wanted to take a chance on him.

"Really," Al affirmed. "I need you to get up here right away. Can you be in Strawberry Point in two days?"

"You bet I can!" Steve exclaimed. He quickly wrote down the directions to the facility and hung up the phone. It was the phone call that would spark the beginning of a new life for Steve.

Al gave Steve the position of assistant manager. Shortly after moving to Chester, Steve got an unexpected visitor: Uncle Glen. He had always had a soft spot in his heart for his nephew Steve because the two shared a middle name and Steve had followed in his footsteps and become a barber. But Glen was still confused about why Steve had left his barber career and family behind in West Union. However, he never demanded answers from Steve.

Glen entered Steve's office in the SMI warehouse and Steve was surprised to see his beloved uncle standing before him once again.

"Uncle Glen!" Steve exclaimed from behind his desk. "What in the world are you doing here?"

"I tracked you down, Steve. I had to come see you. I've been so worried about you," Glen trembled as he spoke. "I'm just so happy to see you are okay."

"I'm okay, Glen," Steve said, hanging his head. "I just haven't seen anyone from the family again, at least not on good terms," Steve added, dejectedly.

"I don't care about all that," Glen insisted, looking Steve straight in the eye. "You are my nephew, my namesake. I love you no matter what," he continued, as tears welled up in his eyes.

With that, Steve jumped up from behind his desk and enveloped his Uncle Glen in a large bear hug.

"I love you, Steve. I can't live without you," Uncle Glen proclaimed.

"I love you too, Uncle Glen," Steve said as tears streamed down his face.

"I don't know what happened or why you left, but I don't care. I just want you to come home. Come back to the family," Glen insisted. "I want you to come visit me in Charles City."

And so the next weekend Steve did just that: he visited his Uncle Glen is Charles City. It was his uncle's complete acceptance and love that helped Steve begin to look at the world in a whole new way.

Two months after starting at the pallet company, manager Virgil Rice took a vacation. While he was gone, company officials looked over the books and found that the numbers didn't add up. When Virgil returned from vacation, they fired him and promoted Steve to manager.

Steve couldn't believe his luck. He was running the place and his confidence was slowly growing. Just a few months ago he had held a gun up to his mouth and had decided not to pull the trigger. He was beginning to believe this really was his new start — a real gift from God. But his challenges weren't over yet. Two weeks after taking on the new role as boss at the plant, Steve got a call in the middle of the night. The warehouse was on fire. Steve leaped out of bed and ran as fast as he could the three blocks over to the building and saw it engulfed in flames.

You've got to be kidding me, God! I get one break in life, and I'm jinxed, again! Steve thought as he helplessly watched the warehouse burn to the ground.

But as bad as the situation was, it turned out that Steve was not jinxed again. Shortly after the fire, authorities determined it was arson. It had been intentionally set by one of the manufacturer's employees. Jerry Jones was arrested and eventually went to prison for the crime. Company officials decided to start over, and put Steve in charge of the project. Steve and two SMI employees were given the job of helping to rebuild the plant.

One day while he was driving the forklift, clearing debris from the ashes of the building, something inside of Steve stirred. He didn't really understand how or why. There was no bolt of lightning, no sudden booming voice from the heavens above. But Steve felt a resolve growing inside of him that he had never felt in his life. He jumped down from the forklift and raised both his hands toward the sky. No one was around, but had anyone been watching him from a distance, they might have figured he had gone crazy.

"God, please forgive me. I will give you another chance! I will go in the direction you want, Lord. But I need your help!" Steve shouted out loud. And with those words Steve asked for forgiveness from God: *"I have sinned — horrible, horrible sins. I know I can't hide any of that from You God. I know You saw it all. I'm so ashamed, God. Please forgive me,"* he asked, as real tears of sorrow and regret streamed down his face.

His mind filled with images of the people he had hurt — his parents, Marlene and his children. He thought about all the drunken nights and the meaningless one-night-stands. For the first time in his life, Steve took complete responsibility for all of it. He was filled with remorse.

"I promise, if You give me another chance, I will not mess it up!" he proclaimed. *"I promise Lord, I will not mess it up ever again!"* he repeated with resolve.

A subtle shift inside of Steve took place, right then and there — a true conversion of his heart. As he climbed back onto the forklift, he felt a sense of peace that truly surpassed all understanding. And then he made another commitment to God: "I will go back to church, Lord, starting this Sunday."

And with that pledge, a nearly instantaneous renewal of Steve's faith would convince him that Christ had always been with him, even through the lowest points in his life and the difficulties yet to come. A few years later he would come across a poem written in 1921 that recapitulated his own spiritual transformation. He memorized each verse and relived his conversion experience every time he spoke these words aloud:

"The Old Violin"
By Myra Brooks Welch

'Twas battered and scarred,

And the auctioneer thought it

hardly worth his while

To waste his time on the old violin,

but he held it up with a smile.

"What am I bid, good people", he cried,

"Who starts the bidding for me?"

"One dollar, one dollar, Do I hear two?"

"Two dollars, who makes it three?"

"Three dollars once, three dollars twice, going for three,"

But, No,

From the room far back a gray bearded man

Came forward and picked up the bow,

Then wiping the dust from the old violin

And tightening up the strings,

He played a melody, pure and sweet

As sweet as the angel sings.

The music ceased and the auctioneer

With a voice that was quiet and low,

Said "What now am I bid for this old violin?"

As he held it aloft with its' bow.

"One thousand, one thousand, Do I hear two?"

"Two thousand, Who makes it three?"

"Three thousand once, three thousand twice,

Going and gone", said he.

The audience cheered,

But some of them cried,

"We just don't understand."

"What changed its' worth?"

Swift came the reply.

"The touch of the Master's Hand."

"And many a man with life out of tune

All battered and bruised with hardship

Is auctioned cheap to a thoughtless crowd

Much like that old violin

A mess of pottage, a glass of wine,

A game and he travels on.

He is going once, he is going twice,

He is going and almost gone.

But the Master comes,

And the foolish crowd never can quite understand,

The worth of a soul and the change that is wrought

By the touch of the Master's Hand.

Chapter 12: An Angel Named Marcella

"She stretcheth out her hand to the poor; yea, she reacheth forth her hands to the needy." Proverbs 31:20

Steve kept his promise and a few days later, when Sunday rolled around, he made the hour drive from Chester to West Union. He didn't plan to go back to the church that he and Marlene had attended. He still couldn't bear to have Pastor Luke's condemning eyes upon him. Instead he picked a small, white, wooden church on the outskirts of town.

The bells were clanging in the tower as he entered Temple Hill Wesleyan Church, and a group of people was coming up from the basement. Among them was a woman he knew named Linda Anderson.

"Steve!" she exclaimed, her shock apparent. "What in the world are you doing here?" she asked.

"I'm going to church!" Steve said with resolve. "I'm going to church," he repeated, leaving Linda looking at him with her mouth gaping open, speechless.

Steve walked into the sanctuary and picked a seat near the back. The preacher was Perry Stevens. Appropriately, his message was about the love of God and how it never fails. Steve realized he didn't feel out of place in this church or even the least bit nervous, even after his encounter with Linda.

As the service ended, Steve got up and made his way toward the door, but a woman stopped him. She was 41-years-old, with wavy, medium-length, sandy blond hair, a broad face and about the softest blue eyes he had ever seen. She had inherited her Scandinavian coloring from her Swedish mother and an Irish twinkle in her eyes from her father. Lines had formed around those eyes from a lifetime of laughter. And when she smiled, she radiated love and warmth to everyone around her.

"Hello there," she sang, her voice, soft and sweet. "My name is Marcella, Marcella Stevens, and I'm the minister's wife. Would you please join us for dinner? Our home is just across the street," she said, beaming at him.

Steve looked at her in surprise. He wasn't used to someone being so kind to him, especially because he was a stranger to Marcella. There was something about this woman that drew him in. He couldn't say no, so he replied, "Why, yes, how kind of you. I'd love to."

And with that, Marcella took his arm and led him down the steps of the church and across the street to the Stevens' home. It was a tiny, two-story brick house with a covered porch in the front. He wasn't prepared for what he would find inside.

Perry and Marcella Stevens had six children, ranging in age from 3 to 20. Marcella had wanted to have twice as many children, but after the sixth, doctors told her that wasn't possible. The second-to-oldest was a young woman named Marie, who looked remarkably like Marcella, but she had long brown hair, parted in the middle, and wore glasses like her father. Marie was 19 and was living at home that summer.

As soon as Steve walked in the door, the smell of a pot roast wafted from the oven, filling his nostrils. His stomach rumbled. Marie was on her way out the door. Marcella stopped her and introduced her to Steve.

"Marie, there's someone I'd like to you meet. This is Steve Frey."

"Hello," Marie said, tersely.

"Hello," Steve mumbled back.

Marie shrugged her shoulders. She was used to her mom bringing strays from the church over for Sunday dinner.

Marie's senior picture

"I've got to go, Mom. I'm supposed to be skydiving today with my friends in Waterloo. I've got to get over there," Marie said impatiently.

"Okay, go ahead, dear. Be careful and we'll see you back home tonight."

Marcella chuckled as Marie bounded out the door.

Skydiving? Steve thought. He looked at Marcella quizzically.

"That's our girl, Marie!" Marcella boasted with obvious pride. "She's quite the adventurous one! Perry was assigned the church here in West Union last spring, and Marie just graduated from high school in Waterloo. She's been going back and forth a lot to see all her friends," Marcella explained.

"Oh, I see," Steve said. And then he peered into the home as laughter from the Stevens' children saturated the kitchen. It was an incredibly happy home, unlike any other he'd ever been in. At that moment, Steve felt as if he actually belonged in the world.

The Stevens family sat around the table, joking and telling stories. Perry was a tall man, with dark hair that was graying around the temples. He wore thick glasses and emitted an inner strength and kindness. His laugh bellowed out through the entire house when his children did something to amuse him. He and Marcella were affectionate and respectful of one another, but often teased each other mercilessly, until Marcella would grab Perry and give him a great big hug and say, "I love you, Mr. Stevens!"

At which point, Perry would reply, "And I you, Mrs. Stevens."

During the next several months, Steve continued to drive to West Union every Sunday for church, which was followed by a big noon dinner at the Stevens' home. Occasionally Marie would also join the family for the meal.

Meanwhile, under Steve's leadership, the pallet company rose from the ashes and flourished. Steve experienced a resurrection from the ashes of his life as well. He traveled around Iowa, taking pallet orders, and the business became more and more successful, eventually reaching about

$2 million in sales over the next three years. Eventually Steve would put that sales experience to use in another capacity, one that he could never have imagined possible at the time.

Steve's appetite for booze and meaningless sex unexplainably subsided, and he replaced it with prayer and the precious moments he spent at the Stevens' home. Marcella constantly demonstrated to him that she was someone who lived out her faith and did what is so difficult for so many: loving others as she loved herself. She accepted people, including Steve, exactly as they were, despite their flaws.

During his Sunday ritual, Steve got to know all the members of the Stevens family very well, and he found himself especially smitten with Marie. She was quick-witted and funny like her father but also sweet and sensible like her mother. She was only 19, and by this time Steve was 30. Despite their age difference, he decided he really wanted to ask her out on a date. But he didn't want to anger Perry or Marcella or risk ruining their friendship, which he had come to value so much. One weekday afternoon, he drove over from Chester and found Perry in his office inside the church building.

"Hello, Perry," Steve said, greeting the pastor as he entered his office.

"Why hello there, Steve. What a pleasant surprise this is!" Perry said, getting up from behind his desk to come around a give Steve a hearty pat on the back.

"What do I owe the honor?" Perry asked him.

"Perry, I want you to know how important your family has become to me. You've taken me in and loved me, just like one of your own. I've been through some difficult times, but thanks to you and your family, my life is getting much, much better," Steve said, thanking him earnestly.

Perry smiled and said, "Well of course, Steve. No thank-you necessary. We enjoy spending time with you."

"Uh," Steve started, not quite sure how to ask the question he came to ask. "I was wondering," Steve started saying, but his voice trailed off.

"What is it Steve? How can I help?" Perry quizzed, raising an eyebrow.

"May I please have your permission to ask your daughter, Marie, on a date?" Steve hurriedly blurted out.

Perry took in a deep breath, but before he had a chance to answer, Steve injected, "I know you may have some hesitation. I know there's a big age difference between us. And I'm sure you've heard about my reputation around West Union. But I want to assure you, I have changed. I am not the same person I was when I used to live here. I will treat Marie with respect. You can trust me with your daughter," Steve pledged, looking anxiously at Perry

Perry looked at him for a long moment, and Steve began to feel uncomfortable in the silence. He looked down at his shoes. Then Perry spoke in soft, measured words. "Steve, I have come to know you over the last several months. My entire family loves you and I do not judge you by your past. However, Marie is precious to us and I can't have you hurting her."

"I promise, I won't!" Steve exclaimed. "Just give me a chance. I really like Marie and my intentions are honorable."

"My answer is yes, then, Steve," Perry said, with a smile forming on his face.

"Oh, thank you, Perry!" Steve said, giddily. "I won't let you down! I will treat Marie right!"

But even with her father's blessing, getting a date with Marie was going to be much harder than Steve anticipated.

Chapter 13: Winning Over Marie
"An excellent wife who can find? She is far more precious than jewels." Proverbs 31:10

While Steve wanted to date Marie, Marie had other ideas. One afternoon following Sunday dinner, Steve asked Marie to take a walk with him. As they strolled down the sidewalk Steve asked, "Marie, will you go out with me Friday night?"

"I'm sorry, Steve. I'm busy," Marie quickly responded.

"How about Saturday, then?" he said.

"Sorry, I already have plans then, too," she replied.

Steve's heart sank. But he didn't give up. Every week Steve would ask Marie out again and she would turn him down — telling him that she already had plans. She had no intention of dating him anyway. He was 11 years her senior and had four children. And even though Steve had been sober for several months, his reputation for hitting the bottle preceded him, and she had no intention of getting involved with someone who drank too much. Marie had been working in a factory in West Union and her coworkers had gossiped quite a bit about Steve's return to town and the trouble he'd been in when he was living there. Most people in town condemned Steve for leaving that *poor woman,* Marlene, all alone with four children.

But Marie was still kind to Steve, even when she turned him down. She knew her parents were helping him and that he was trying to stay sober, and she didn't want to mess that up. Steve asked her out three times in a row. By his fourth attempt, he had a new plan. "I know you're busy this weekend, right?" Steve asked Marie.

"Yep," she replied.

"And I have plans next weekend. You probably have plans then, too, right?" he asked.

"Yep," she replied again.

"Now the third weekend, let's plan something for that Saturday night." Steve said.

Marie knew she was backed into a corner now. She either had to say yes or tell him she didn't want to date him at all and she was worried about letting him down. *What if that drove him to drink?* she wondered.

"Oh, okay. I guess that works," she said.

That night she told her mother that she had reluctantly accepted a date with Steve.

"He's a nice young man," Marcella told Marie. "He won't hurt you. You be nice to him."

And so she was. Two months after he had first started asking her out, Steve drove to her house on a Saturday night to pick her up. Perry was standing in the doorway, and Steve walked up to shake his hand. Marie came down the stairs wearing a striped blouse and blue polyester slacks. To Steve, she was the most gorgeous woman he had ever seen. And it wasn't just how she looked. Marie was even more beautiful on the inside. That's something that Steve never would have recognized in his younger years.

"Take good care of her, Steve," Perry warned, as the couple walked toward the door.

"Of course," Steve replied. And he *really* meant it.

Then, several of the little Stevens boys began to chime in.

"Marie, Marie, can we go, too? We want malts," five-year-old Andy pleaded.

"Yeah, Maaarie," three-year-old Charley whined. "*I wanna mawlt too, pease*," Charley begged.

"No, boys, you can't go with us," Marie said, laughing.

"But we will bring you back malts — both of you," Steve promised.

"I want chocolate," Andy said.

"*And I wanna vaneeela!*" Charley proclaimed.

"Okay, okay, boys!" Steve said, chuckling.

Steve was still driving that old Pontiac. It had one long bench seat in the front. Steve opened the door for Marie and she got in the car. Perry was peering at them through the window. Marie was nervous and sat as close to the door as possible. Steve wondered if she might jump out if he slowed down. She didn't want Steve to get any ideas. She'd really only gone out with him to make her mother happy. Steve drove Marie to a steakhouse in McGregor, Iowa about 45 minutes away. The meal went much better than Marie expected. Steve made her laugh over and over again, and she decided maybe he wasn't such a bad guy after all. Then at her insistence they stopped at a drive-in on the way home to pick up milk shakes for her little brothers.

Marie agreed to go on a second date with Steve the following weekend. When he picked her up, once again, Perry was standing at the door. This time he said, "Order the lobster, Marie. See if this guy is a cheapskate!"

Steve chuckled. That night the couple drove to Waterloo to Red Lobster for dinner. She even brought home the shell to show her dad. Steve and Marie began to spend more and more time together. Marie thought Steve was both funny and fun, and he gave her plenty of space. Marie wasn't ready yet for anything more. But the two began to develop a deep friendship. Steve was patient and never pushed himself on her. He also didn't want to jeopardize his relationship with Perry and Marcella.

Marie worked the nightshift at the factory in West Union and got off at midnight. Steve would join her and her coworkers after work hanging out at different people's houses. Sometimes they would build a bonfire and roast hot dogs. And while someone might have had a beer or two at the get-togethers, they seldom included alcohol. Steve stayed strong, never falling off the wagon.

One day Marie and Perry showed up at Steve's office in Chester to pick him up to go out for dinner. Steve had about 10 sales contracts to sign and hurriedly scribbled his name on each document: *Steven W. Frey, Steven W. Frey, Steven W. Frey.*

After the third one, Perry peered at his signature. "What's the "W" stand for?" he asked.

Steve was about to tell them it stood for Woodrow and that he was named after his Uncle Glen. But before Steve had a chance to answer, Marie interjected. "I know," she giggled. "It stands for Wiener! He looks like a Wiener to me!"

At this point she burst into laughter and Perry joined in. Steve couldn't help but chuckle himself. And from that day on, "Wiener" became Marie's pet name for Steve. In fact, Marie's entire family stopped calling him Steve and he became known as Wiener to all of them.

Marie & Steve

While he was courting Marie, Steve would drive to Colorado to pick up his four children and bring them back to Iowa to stay with him. He told Marie, "I've got four kids that I love very much. Being with me also means being with my kids.

If you're not ready for that, I understand. But if that's the case, I also have to move on."

Marie did love Steve's children, though, almost immediately after she met them. But she was still uncertain about taking on the role of stepmother at just 19. She also worried that Steve and Marlene perhaps did really belong together. She thought if there was any chance that the couple, who shared four children together would reconcile, she shouldn't stand in the way. However, more than a year after they started dating, Steve wanted Marie to marry him. He even bought her a ring.

One evening he picked her up and after he got in the car, he asked her to marry him.

"I don't think I want to get married right now. I don't think you're my prince charming," Marie told him after he showed her the ring. Marie really didn't feel ready to get married. She didn't feel that Steve had been sober long enough, either. But Steve wasn't deterred easily. He figured he could wear her down, the same way he had finally gotten her to agree to go on a date with him.

"I think I could change your mind," Steve told her. "I'll wait as long as it takes," he promised. And he hung the ring from the turn signal knob next to the steering wheel in his Pontiac. Every weekend when he picked her up for a date, Steve would say, "Are you ready for the ring yet?"

And Marie would reply, "No, Wiener, not yet."

Her "not yet" was all the encouragement Steve needed. "Not yet" didn't mean "no." And while it didn't mean "yes," either, it still gave Steve the hope he needed to keep asking.

* * *

Marcella began losing consciousness and hearing voices in her head. At one point, Marcella believed the devil was chasing her. One evening she blacked out and Perry called an ambulance, which took her to Waterloo to the hospital. A brain scan didn't reveal the problem, so Marcella was transferred to Mayo Clinic in Rochester, Minnesota, where doctors ordered an MRI. They discovered that Marcella had a tumor the size of a lemon above her right temple. She underwent emergency surgery and spent the next several months recovering at home.

Marie and Perry took turns driving Marcella the 100 miles to and from Rochester for radiation therapy. It was a nasty winter and the ordeal was tough on the family. Marie began to rely more and more on Steve for support to get through her mother's illness. Marcella was plagued by memory loss and seizures for years following the surgery and radiation.

Marie and her sister Lisa, Mother Marcella and other sister, Sandy

A year after her mother's surgery, Steve said to Marie, "I'm getting too emotionally involved with you. I love you, Marie. You either have to marry me or I have to leave and not come back because I don't want to get hurt again."

Marie looked into his eyes a good long while. Then she sighed and said, "Wiener, I'd marry you, but I'm not ready. I'm really not, and I don't think that's right to pressure me like this when I'm not ready. I do love you. I'm just not ready."

But Steve wasn't willing to accept that answer, completely. Three months later, he called the Stevens' former church in Waterloo and booked two available dates for their wedding; June 12 and June 19 of 1982, even though Marie hadn't even said yes — *yet.*

He told the woman on the phone that he would call back next week and let her know what date he would take. Then he drove 65 miles to West Union to Marie's house. When he pulled up, she came storming out.

What's this about us getting married in June?" Marie said demandingly to Steve, scowling at him as he got out of the car. "I heard that from my mother! You'd better have a good explanation, Wiener!" Her tone even made her cute little nickname for him sound bad.

Marcella was hurt because she believed that Marie hadn't told her the two were getting married and had already chosen a date. Unbeknownst to Steve, Marcella's mother, Marie's grandmother, was on the wedding committee at the church had called Marcella when she heard her granddaughter's wedding was coming up and no one had told her.

"Marie," Steve began. "If we *were* to get married in June, which date would you take, the 12th or the 19th?"

"Well," Marie said, taking a deep breath. "It would have to be the 19th, because I'm in my friend Vickie's wedding on the 12th."

"Okay!" Steve exclaimed. The 19th is good for me." And with that, he jumped back in his car and drove away before she had the chance to say no.

Marie went into the house and told Marcella that Steve had booked the church without her knowledge.

"He's a good man. You'll be fine with each other. You should say yes, Marie," Marcella said in her soft-spoken, gentle way. Marie respected her mother's opinion and didn't want to let her down.

So the next week, Marie did say yes, and Steve took the small diamond ring he had purchased off the turn signal and placed it on Marie's finger while they were sitting in the car. Steve was the happiest he'd ever been in his life. It was at that point that Marie knew for certain then that she loved him and his children, and she was now firmly committed to all of them.

The couple was married on June 19, 1982. Marie's entire family was part of the wedding. Steve's cousin, Al, who got him the job in Chester, stood up for him. The only other

Marcella, Marie & Perry

member of the Frey family who attended was Steve's Uncle Glen. No one else would come to the ceremony because they didn't approve of Steve getting divorced, and they certainly wouldn't support him marrying another woman.

A lot of stories had floated around West Union and had gotten back to the Frey family. They saw Marie as a homewrecker. But in reality, nothing could have been further from the truth. In fact, that was one of the reasons Marie and put Steve off for so long. In her firm resolve to follow her faith, Marie had remained virtuous until their wedding night.

Marie and Steve Frey Wed on June 18, 1982

Nine years after Steve and Marie were married, Marcella's seizures got worse because the tumor was back. One day Perry was watching TV and saw an ad on for a brain surgeon at a hospital in Des Moines. He got Marcella an appointment, but the news wasn't good. That doctor told her there was no hope in eliminating the new tumor that had grown in her brain, but he was willing to drain it to take off the pressure.

The tumor continued to grow, and Marcella lost her ability to speak. She would just babble and no one could understand her. Marie would travel home during this period of Marcella's illness and spent a great deal of time just holding her. She took care of her, gently bathing Marcella, brushing her teeth and combing her hair. The family kept her at home for as long as possible, but eventually moved her into a nursing home in Marshalltown, Iowa for the last month of her life. Perry had been assigned a new church there. Marcella's memory was fading fast; she couldn't remember the names of her family members. But every time Steve came to see her, a funny look came over her face and she squealed, "Wiener!"

Even in the end, Marcella was still trying to help others. While she was in the nursing home, she had a roommate named Lucille, who complained all the time about how she felt and the fact she was in the nursing home. Marcella was just 85 pounds and couldn't even get out of bed. But one night, while Lucille was complaining about being cold, Marcella managed to reach for a small gold cross at her bedside. Then she reached out and pulled off her blanket and tried to push her blanket toward Lucille, but it landed on the floor instead.

Lucille looked over at Marcella. "What?" Lucille barked.

Marcella couldn't speak, but she opened her tightly clenched fist to show Lucille the gold cross. A few days later, Marcella died peacefully at just 48. Her death shook Steve to his very core. He felt closer to Marcella than his own mother. Marcella had never judged him and had loved him and everybody she met unconditionally. Steve sobbed so uncontrollably at her funeral that Marie thought she might have to take him out of the church. Marcella had taught Steve the true meaning of unconditional love and had helped change his life. Never again would Steve know a woman so kind, loving and compassionate. Marcella radiated beauty, inside and out, and just being in her presence had calmed him. The only other woman who came close to having all those qualities was Marcella's daughter, Marie. And Steve had married her.

Chapter 14: A Second Chance at Love

"A wife of noble character who can find? She is worth far more than rubies." Proverbs 31:10

Steve borrowed $1,000 to buy a mobile home after he and Marie got married. They put the home in the New Hampton trailer court located between Chester and West Union. The couple both drove about 40 miles each way to their respective jobs. Most of Marie's paycheck at the factory went for Steve's child support payment. They had a wood-burning stove in the middle of the mobile home. It was so cold in that mobile home in the winter that their toilet water often froze.

Steve continued to see his children, especially in the summers when he brought them to stay with him. But life was still not easy for him and Marie. Between their lack of money and the scorn of the small community, they both endured, some days could be really tough. On one particularly rough day, Steve was sitting on the steps of the mobile home with Jeremiah, who was 5 at the time. Steve was lost in thought and became overwhelmed with self-pity and tears began to run down his face. He looked down at little Jeremiah, whom he suddenly realized had been staring at him intently, and noticed that he was also crying.

"What's wrong, Jeremiah?" Steve asked, as he put his hand on the boy's shoulder.

"Daddy, when you're sad, I'm sad. And when you're happy, I'm happy," Jeremiah exclaimed through his tears.

"Oh, Jeremiah!" Steve said, tenderly putting his arms around the boy. "Then I'm not going to be unhappy anymore because all I want for you is to be happy!" Then Steve forced a smile onto his face.

"Really, Daddy?"

"You bet!" Steve assured him. "Let's go get some ice cream!"

Zachariah, Jeremiah, Dinah & Hannah Frey with their half-brother, David

Jeremiah's tender heart never hardened. He would grow up and met his wife, Kelley, in Denver, and the two would become missionaries in Mexico. Jeremiah is credited with starting three successful churches in Guadalajara and bringing them into the World Wide Mission. Today, Jeremiah helps oversee 24 churches for the organization in Mexico.

Meanwhile, Steve continued to work at the pallet company for another two years. But he was getting restless and began searching for another position. Eventually he was offered a job as production manager of grand pianos at the Baldwin Piano Company in Conway, Arkansas. Al Frey never did understand why Steve wanted to leave the pallet company, since it was doing so well. But Steve was ready for a new challenge, and in this job he would oversee 300 employees. Marie was willing to move as well, because her factory job wasn't holding her there and her dad had taken on a new church in Marshalltown, Iowa. Marie was able to secure another factory job in Arkansas.

While they were living there, Steve called Harley and begged him to come and visit. But Harley and Berneice never would come to see them while they were in Arkansas. However, even though all the Freys had made it clear they didn't approve of Steve's divorce or of him marrying Marie, that didn't stop them from asking for money from Steve and Marie.

One day after Harley and Berneice had moved to Platte, South Dakota, Berneice called Steve and said, "Steve, your father wants to start a restaurant with your sister, Ruth, and her husband, Chuck, on Main Street. But he needs some money. Do you have any money we can borrow?"

Steve couldn't believe his ears. After how his family had shunned him, now they wanted money! It took everything in him to hold back what he really wanted to say. "I'll have to check with Marie and get back to you," Steve told his mother.

That evening, when Marie returned home from work, Steve told her about his conversation with his mother. "I can't believe the nerve!" Steve said to Marie, "They wouldn't come to our wedding. They've never been here to visit, and now they want us to give them money!"

Marie looked at Steve for a long moment. She took a deep breath and then she spoke. "Wiener, somebody has to make the first move," she said. "Someone has to be kind to heal this rift in your family. I think it should be us."

"What do you mean, Marie?" Steve asked. "We don't have any money!"

"Remember when I left the factory and I took my retirement fund with me?"

"Yeah," Steve said, looking at her skeptically.

"I know it's only three thousand dollars, but we could give them that."

"You've got to be kidding me?" Steve said, incredulously. "No one has treated you worse than my family. And now you want to give them the little bit of savings you have?"

"I do, Wiener," Marie continued. "It's time to mend fences with your family. We're going to send your dad the money." Marie spoke with a firm resolve.

Steve knew better than to argue. "Okay," Steve said, sighing. "But they don't deserve it."

"That doesn't matter," Marie said.

The next day, Steve wrote out a check on the couple's joint checking account for $3,000. With that money, Harley and Steve's youngest sister, Ruth, and her husband, Chuck Anholt, opened a restaurant called the Aristocrat Café in an old bank building on Main Street in Platte. The sign out front was of a penguin in a waiter's costume. The Aristocrat served traditional, small town fare: hot beef sandwiches and big breakfasts.

Three years later, Harley had to go in for open-heart surgery. He was preparing for the worst and made a list of everyone he owed money. He had written out an IOU to Steve for $3,000. Berneice looked at it and said to him, "Harley, why did you write out an IOU to Steve?"

"It's that money I owe him from starting the café," Harley replied.

"That wasn't Steve's money. He didn't give that to you. Marie did," Berneice told him.

Harley was shocked. He had always assumed it was Steve who sent the money. He couldn't believe that Marie had been willing to give him the money, after all, he and Berneice had nothing to do with her and had made it clear they disapproved of the couple's marriage.

After he came out of surgery, Steve and Marie were in Harley's hospital room in Sioux Falls, South Dakota. The couple had driven through the night from Arkansas to be by his side.

Harley motioned for Marie to approach him. She leaned over closer to him as he whispered, "Thank you, Marie," Harley croaked. "I'm going to pay you back."

"Oh no, you're not," Marie said adamantly. "We're family and you don't owe me anything."

For a man who was never left speechless in his life, Harley was at a loss for words. A single tear rolled down his cheek and from that day on a bond between Harley and Marie was formed.

Steve and Marie didn't stay in Arkansas for long. Steve had heard about a job in Milwaukee with All Glass Aquarium as a factory superintendent. While there, Steve designed an all-wooden case to enclose the fish aquariums to make them look more like furniture. He oversaw the installation of the machinery to do the woodworking, assembly and painting of the casing. The company patented Steve's design. It even earned him a prestigious award one year for the coming up with the best new product in the pet industry.

Marie got a job at Junior House Collectibles, which later changed its name to JH Collectibles. The company had a fancy showroom in New York; Cindy Crawford and Christie Brinkley modeled the clothing line. Marie's job was to give final approval to garments before they left the factory.

Marcella passed away while the couple was living in Wisconsin. At the time, Marie's little brother Charley was 16 and Perry was suffering from depression at the loss of his wife. Charley had been staying out all night with his friends and Perry felt he was in no condition to handle another rebellious teenager. Perry had also lost his mother at a young age and spent many years alone with his father. He didn't want the same fate for Charley, as it hadn't been pleasant for him. Perry asked Steve and Marie if Charley could come stay with them in Steven's Point, Wisconsin. They agreed, and a few weeks later they had a teenage boy living with them.

Marie became Charley's mother figure and the two had a very close bond. Charley was pretty easy-going and didn't mind going to stay with Marie and Steve. In fact, he welcomed a change of scenery and making new friends. Charley spent many of his summers in recent years at Steve's and Marie's. His mother had been ill for half of his life, and he welcomed a reprieve from sickness and death. Marie and Steve filled a void for Charley and helped instill in him a hard-work ethic.

Marie and Steve worked long days, and they expected Charley to work as well. Marie got Charley a job before school at a Dressage Barn, where Trakehner horses were trained for show. Then, after school, Charley worked at a car wash. One of Charley's memories from that time was waking up at 4:30 in the morning to drive Steve to a Perkin's restaurant, where he would sit and watch Steve drink coffee and read the paper, until Steve was ready for Charley to drive him to work. If Charley wanted to use a car for the day, he was expected to take part in this ritual. Charley stayed on with them for two years, until he graduated from high school. Then he joined the U.S. Navy, where he volunteered for the submarine training program.

But the bond remained among the three, and Charley was more of a child to Steve and Marie. Charley visited them while on leave from the Navy. And even years later, after he ended up living in Australia, he always made a trip home to the Freys, his surrogate parents. Ironically, later on, Charley, Steve and Marie ended up in the consumer packaged-goods industry.

Every summer, Steve would make the annual trip to Colorado to pick up his four children and drive them back to where he and Marie were living. But as Dinah got a little older, she questioned whether Steve loved her, since he had left long before she was even born.

"Daddy, why did you leave me? Don't you love me, Daddy," a six-year-old Dinah said, looking up at Steve with her big blue eyes welling with tears.

"Of course I do — you're my little Din-ah-mite!" Steve said affectionately, tearing up himself. But he knew he hadn't convinced her by the way she averted her eyes from his.

Dinah spent much of her childhood wondering if she really had her father's love. But all four Frey children took to Marie almost immediately, calling her "Ree." And "Ree" had made a promise to herself and to Steve to love his children as her own. She'd worked hard to develop a relationship with them while she and Steve were dating. In fact, she made a conscious decision not to get pregnant, because she felt four children were enough, and Steve agreed. Shortly after they were married, during one of Steve's visitation times, Marie sat all four children down and said, "I just want you to know, I had to marry your dad because I fell in love with all of you kids!" Then she wrapped her arms around the children and gave them a big group hug. Marie's relationship with the four Frey children has always been among the most important ones in her life.

While Steve and Marie both had to go to work during the days, when his children stayed with them in the summers, they both made an effort to do fun activities with the kids during the evenings and on weekends. To this day, Dinah remembers Steve taking all four children on tours of the factories he managed. The smell of manufacturing is something that can bring her right back to those days where she felt so proud of her dad. Then Steve would treat the kids to a soda out of the company vending machine.

Steve wasn't above embarrassing his children either. Dinah watched one summer as Steve attempted to teach her brothers how to play tennis. Steve was barking out orders, running all over the court wearing tube socks and short running shorts with white stripes on the side. *My dad is such a dork!* Dinah thought. The Freys took the kids to Milwaukee Brewers' games, and they all collected baseball cards.

When those summers would come to an end, Steve would load the children back in the car and make the long drive to Colorado. As he approached Littleton, tears would stream down his cheeks. His children would always remember how hard it was for their dad to drop them back off at their mother's home. Steve thought to himself that it was the terrible price he had to pay for the sins of his past.

Steve and Marie had also purchased an old fire truck at an auction. Marie loved to give the kids in the neighborhood rides on that truck, with sirens blaring. It was the highlight of the summer for Steve's children. Charley even drove it to school a time or two. But if he was up too late playing music, he could count on Marie blaring the horns at the crack of dawn, just to get back at him!

Meanwhile, Steve called up his Uncle Glen one day while living in Wisconsin, but found a very grumpy man on the other end of the line.

"What do you mean, *Uncle* Glen? I think I'm just Glen to you now, Steve!"

"What in the world are you talking about, *Uncle* Glen?" Steve implored, stressing the word "uncle."

"You don't have any time for me anymore! I never see you!"

"Ah," Steve understood. His aging uncle was feeling neglected. Glen has many of his own troubles and Steve decided not to take it personally. But every time he called Glen over the next year, he seemed angry, which was devastating to Steve, who saw his uncle as someone who had always truly cared for him and helped him turn his life around. Steve prayed for his uncle every day and eventually he got this letter from him:

Dear Steven,

 You know I don't want you to still be angry with me when we meet in Heaven. I'm saying right now whatever I said or did to you, I'm sorry. I didn't mean to do anything wrong. I ask your forgiveness and let's start where we left off a couple years ago.
 Your Uncle Glen

 Steve immediately went to go visit Glen in Charles City, Iowa, and the uncle and nephew recaptured their close relationship until the day Glen Woodrow Frey died at the age of 88 in 2001, a little over a year after Steve received his letter.

 About once a year, Steve and Marie heard from Steve's parents. It remained difficult for Steve to deal with the fact that his parents and sisters refused to come to his wedding to Marie and had condemned him for getting divorced from Marlene. Steve's family had taken Marlene's side and had done what **they** could to help his children. And the separation from his son had changed Harley. The once outgoing, vivacious preacher had become quiet and withdrawn.

 While Steve wasn't angry, he was hurt. **He** tried to move past it and focus on his job and his marriage. When he did get the occasional phone call from Harley and Berneice, it was usually because they wanted to know when they could see their grandchildren, Steve's children. He always hung up the phone feeling down rather than uplifted. For years, he didn't hear anything at all from his sisters Janice, Diane or Ruth. They were all under the false impression that Marie had broken up Steve's marriage to Marlene and refused to believe differently.

Chapter 15: The Visit that Changed Everything

"May the God of endurance and encouragement grant you to live in such harmony with one another, in accord with Christ Jesus, that together you may with one voice glorify the God and Father of our Lord Jesus Christ." Romans 15:5-6

Despite the lack of communication and hard feelings that lingered, the bonds of family compelled Steve to keep trying to reestablish a connection to his parents. So, one weekend Steve and Marie made the long car trip to Platte to spend the Thanksgiving holiday with the Freys. The visit went remarkably well, and Steve felt it was an answer to his prayers. Just as the couple was about to leave, Harley followed Steve out to his car as he loaded the luggage. Marie had remained inside, talking to Berneice and Ruth.

"Steve, there's something I need to say," Harley announced. And Steve heard a vigor in his voice that reminded him of the days the congregation had called him "Hollerin' Harley." Since his heart surgery his father seemed much more frail, a shadow of the man who once commanded the pulpit.

"What is it, Dad?" Steve said, setting the suitcase in the trunk and turning to his father.

"I love you, son." Harley said sincerely. "I know you've been waiting to hear that for several years and my disappointment in you made it impossible for me to say it. But the truth is, I never stopped loving you. You are my only son. I want you to come home."

Harley opened his arms and Steve fell into them crying, as the two men hugged. In an instant, all the hard feelings the two had harbored against one another vanished.

On the drive back to Wisconsin, Steve turned to Marie in the passenger seat and said, "Marie, I've been thinking — and I don't want you to get angry," he began.

Marie turned her head to look at him, realizing by his demeanor that Steve was about to saying something that could change the course of their lives. "Go ahead, Wiener. Whatever it is, just say it," she said.

"Marie, it's time. It's time to move home," he proclaimed.

"Why?" Marie questioned, stunned. The announcement seemed to come out of left field. While she'd also been encouraged by how pleasant his parents had been to her during the visit, she certainly wasn't expecting this. And she had been put off by Ruth and Chuck, who in her mind were still giving them the cold shoulder.

"My dad is getting old. I think it's my duty to go home and help him. Please just think about it," Steve pleaded.

"Okay, I will think about it, Wiener." Marie understood that Steve wanted a chance to make things right with his family. But she wasn't yet convinced that could actually happen.

The couple arrived back in Wisconsin, and the following day went to their respective jobs. Three months went by and neither made any mention of that conversation in the car.

In the meantime, the Freys had expanded the Aristocrat Café in Platte and had asked for money from Steve and Marie to buy a truck for home deliveries. They wanted the truck to deliver the now, locally known pies and ice cream the Freys made and served in the restaurant. Harley and Berneice were even selling their homemade ice cream, which they called Aristo, at the Crazy Horse Monument in the Black Hills and at the Pioneer Auto Museum in Murdo, South Dakota. Harley always called it the "best ice cream in the world." The secret to its flavor was that unlike most soft serve ice cream that had four percent butter fat, Aristo Ice Cream had 14 percent butterfat. They had used all their own money to buy ice cream dipping cabinets for the various locations that carried their product. A few small town grocery stores had also agreed to sell their frozen treat.

Berneice was never much of a cook, but she liked to bake and her old-fashioned pies were as authentic as could be, right down to the lard crust and real fruit fillings. They were popular for home deliveries. Harley had started making the ice cream to accompany the pies. Marie told Steve they should send them the $1,200 the couple had saved.

And while the two hadn't talked again about moving to Platte to help the family business, it was on the forefront of both of their minds. Marie was the kind of person who always wanted to do the right thing. After months of going back and forth in her mind, considering just what the right thing was in this situation, Marie told Steve she was ready to give him her answer. Putting her reservations aside about Ruth's and Chuck's attitudes toward them, she told Steve: "Life goes pretty fast, and you don't know how much time you really have. Your parents are getting older and if your family wants to make things right with you, I'm not going to stand in the way of that. We can move to Platte, if that's what you think is best," she acquiesced.

While Marie wasn't thrilled about the prospect of moving to the small town, she didn't let Steve see that. He jumped up at her words and grabbed her and hugged her.

"I love you, Marie! I know it's a lot to ask, but this is going to be the best decision. I just know it!" he proclaimed.

"But I do have one condition, Wiener," Marie said, "I'm not working in that restaurant!"

The Aristocrat Café hadn't been doing as well for the Freys at this point as the outside sales of pies and ice cream.

"I know just what we need to do!" Steve proclaimed. And with that, he picked up the phone to call Harley.

"Dad," he said upon hearing his dad's voice on the other end of the line, "Marie and I are willing to move to Platte. But you have to agree to close the restaurant and focus on making pies and ice cream. Marie and I will help you and mom, and we will come up with a business plan," Steve said.

There was a long pause on the other end of the phone as Harley processed everything Steve had just said to him. "Alright, Steve. The Aristocrat is draining our accounts anyway. I think you're right. We need to close it. And we will work together on that business plan," Harley said. "And, son, he continued, "I'm so happy you're coming home."

Steve placed the receiver back on the cradle and turned to Marie, "I am so blessed to have you as my wife, Marie. Thank you."

Marie wrapped her arms around him and whispered in his ear, "It's the right thing to do."

Chapter 16: A Slice of the Pie
"And let the beauty of the LORD *our God be upon us: and establish thou the work of our hands upon us; yea, the work of our hands establish thou it."* Psalm 90:17

The first thing Steve and Marie did upon arriving in Platte was to pay a visit to the School of Business at the University of South Dakota in Vermillion to get help coming up with a business plan. The plan included shutting down the Aristocrat Café and turning the old bank building on Main Street into a commercial kitchen to bake the pies and make Aristo ice cream. Ruth wasn't keen on closing the restaurant, but acquiesced to her father's wishes.

While a handful of small-town grocery stores were carrying Berneice's pies, they wanted to get them into some of the bigger grocers as well. They named the company Aristo Industries Incorporated. Berneice and Harley, Ruth and Chuck, as well as Steve and Marie were all named officers in the new corporation in January 1990.

Steve and Harley loaded some of Berneice's homemade pies into Harley's white Lincoln Continental and made the two-hour drive to Sioux Falls. Their first stop was a Hy-Vee Grocery Store. Steve asked to see the frozen-food manager, whose name was Todd Holflock. He introduced himself to the manager, showed him a pie and told him, "I want to sell this pie in your store."

Todd took a look at pie in Steve's hand, which was in a plain, white baker's box, and shrugged. "I'm afraid that would be tough," Todd said.

"Why's that?" Steve asked, as Harley looked on.

"It doesn't have a UPC code. It doesn't have a list of ingredients or anything on there," Todd said.

"If I put the ingredients on it, design a box and put a UPC code on it, will you sell them?" Steve asked.

"Sure," Todd said, not thinking for a minute that he'd ever lay eyes on Steve or Harley again.

The two men got in their car and headed back toward Platte.

"Dad," Steve said to Harley, "I am going to figure out how to get a UPC code and I'll design the box. Don't worry!"

After they arrived home, Steve told his mother he needed her picture for the front of the pie box. Berneice obliged and stood against the brick wall in the old bank building, as Marie took her picture.

Then Marie helped design the cover of the box with Berneice's portrait. Steve found a company to print UPC code stickers and sent away for them. Then they came up with name for the product: *Grandma Frey's Homemade Pies.*

Two weeks later, Steve and Harley made the journey back to the Sioux Falls Hy-Vee store with their newly designed box, complete with a UPC code, in hand. They asked for Todd, who was surprised to see them back so soon.

"I've designed the box, listed the ingredients and have a UPC code," Steve told him. "Now we'll bring my mother in and you can set her up here in the store and she can bake pies and pass out samples to your customers," Steve announced.

Todd looked at the two men incredulously. People wanting to sell their homemade food often approached him, but few of them were industrious enough to actually follow through with the steps necessary to get the product on the grocery store shelf. Harley and Steve were the exception. And he *had* told them he would give the pies a shot if they had everything needed.

"Okay, then," Todd said, honoring his word. "Bring your mother in on Saturday morning and we'll see how it goes"

The ride home was a joyful one for Harley and Steve as they celebrated this victory together. They were both convinced that once a big store like Hy-Vee carried *Grandma Frey's Homemade Pies*, they would be well on their way to getting the pies into many other grocery stores as well.

Saturday arrived and Steve, Harley, Marie and Berneice woke up at the crack of dawn to get the pies ready and make the trip to the Sioux Falls Hy-Vee store. They loaded the huge trunk of Harley's Lincoln full of Berneice's pies: apple, apple-rhubarb, strawberry-rhubarb and peach. When they got to Hy-Vee, they backed the car up to the rear doors and Todd came out. As they opened the trunk, the number of pies inside shocked him.

"You'll never sell all those," Todd said.

"Oh yes we will," proclaimed Harley. "You just wait and see! We will sell every last one."

Berneice, Marie, Steve and Harley began loading the pies into shopping carts and took them into the store, where they set up a table, complete with a portable oven, to give out samples of warm pie. Berneice's sweet disposition and grandmotherly manners got most customers to pause, as they noticed her picture on the pie box. Once they sampled the baked good, they almost always put a pie in their shopping cart. The Freys sold almost all the pies on that Saturday. They returned to the store on Sunday and sold every last pie they had. They cost about a dollar more than other frozen pies in the store, but that didn't discourage customers because of the superior homemade taste.

A few weeks later, Steve was handing out pie samples in the Empire Hy-Vee in Sioux Falls, when a well-dressed man came up to him and asked for a piece. A few minutes later he came back for another.

"Hey," Steve said, jokingly, "if you're going to eat that much, why not buy a whole pie? You won't regret it!"

"I think you're right! That is an excellent pie," the man said, laughing. Then he introduced himself, "I'm Ken Stevens. I'm the district manager for the all Hy-Vee stores in this area. Take your pies to my other Hy-Vee stores and tell them I said they need to carry it!"

"Okay!" Steve replied, excitedly. And before he knew it, *Grandma Frey's Homemade Pies* were in 35 Hy-Vee stores in northwest Iowa, southwest Minnesota, all of South Dakota and northern Nebraska.

While the pies were taking off, every week the Freys also delivered ice cream to all the locations that carried Aristo across South Dakota. Eventually, they were making up to 1,500 gallons of ice cream a week. Marie had offered to help Harley make the ice cream. The two spent hours each week in the kitchen getting it ready. They stirred sugar, cream and milk in large vats until the sugar dissolved and a foam ring appeared around the edge. After that, it was ready for the flavoring. Then they would chill that mixture overnight and the next day transfer it to ice cream machines. Years of factory work made Marie quite adept at the job. But Marie also wanted to get to know Harley better because he'd been such a central figure in Steve's life.

After the success of the pies, the Hy-Vee stores also agreed to carry Aristo Ice Cream. One day Marie agreed to drive Harley to the Brookings, South Dakota Hy-Vee store to hand out ice cream samples. After a couple of hours, Marie told Harley to take a break and began handing out the samples herself. Harley wasn't sure how good Marie would be at this task, so he lurked in the aisle next to where the sample table was located and listened as customers approached Marie.

Later that night, Harley announced to the family as they gathered for dinner, "Marie is quite the salesperson! She is very good!"

Marie blushed, but she was pleased. She had *finally* won Harley over. The two formed such a strong bond they eventually called each other their "best friend."

Berneice, on the other hand, never really warmed up to Marie and wasn't able to ever fully trust Steve again. She couldn't get over the past and forgive him the way Harley did. Even though she worked side by side with Steve in the business, she was always guarded around him, and it felt to Steve as if there was an invisible wall of stone between them. Berneice relied on Harley to be the peacemaker in the family and didn't take any steps to reconcile with Steve herself.

While they were building the pie and ice cream business, out of the blue Charley called Marie. He announced he'd met a girl while stationed at Pearl Harbor and was moving to her homeland of Australia.

"Marie," Charley said, as the line crackled during the long-distance landline call, "I've got to get a job. The Navy taught me to do three things really well. I can shoot an M-16, I can dive, and I can drive a submarine. What I am going to do here?

"Charley," Marie began. "I'll tell you what. Call Sarah Lee. Sarah Lee has operations all over the world, including Australia. Marie had learned this at the trade shows she and Steve frequented. Tell them you're an account manager for us."

"What's an account manager?" Charley asked.

"You'll figure it out from there," Marie assured him.

And that's exactly what Charley did. He called up Sarah Lee's manufacturing facility in Pymble and got his first job in the corporate world as an account manager in charge of a small Australian retailer. It was the start of Charley's climb up the corporate world, which would eventually lead him a top position with CoverGirl/Max Factor for the Asian-Pacific region.

Meanwhile, within three years, *Grandma Frey's Homemade Pies* made their way into more Hy-Vee stores, including ones in Omaha and Des Moines. Steve, Marie, Harley and Berneice were each working up to 20 hours a day. As the business grew, there were some days when they would go on just an hour or two of sleep. Ruth kept track of the books and her husband

Steve & Marie in front of the old bank building

Chuck drove the company's delivery trucks. The Freys had hired 10 employees to turn out 1,500 pies a day from the old bank building. The next step was figuring out how to warehouse them.

They also tapped into the Minneapolis market. The upscale grocer Lunds & Byerlys agreed to carry *Grandma Frey's*. Steve and Marie spent the month of November in Minneapolis traveling from store to store to sell the pies. They would set up their ovens in the entryway of the Lunds & Byerlys store in the suburb of Wayzata, Minnesota, and it became such a holiday tradition in the days leading up to Thanksgiving that eventually they were selling a pie every thirty seconds.

In addition to traveling all over several Midwestern states to promote their pies in the grocery stores, the Freys attended big regional food shows where the *Grandma Frey's Homemade Pies'* booth was set up right next to *Sarah Lee,* the leading pie manufacturer in the country. That was when both Steve and Marie knew that they'd made it big. Topco out of Chicago, a private brand labeler, approached the Freys about making a private label pie for the company.

At the height of the business, they produced 2,500 pies day out of Platte, South Dakota. All the while, Harley and Berneice lived in the basement of the old bank building where they made the pies. Zachariah, Steve's oldest son, also ended up helping out with the pie business for a time. Zach had completed a couple of years of college, but wasn't sure which direction to take in his life and decided to take a break. Steve and Marie invited Zach to live with them, and he spent more than a year in Platte. So three generations of Frey men were working side by side, all to make the business a success. Steve and Marie enjoyed their time with Zach, and he took to small-town life by coaching little league and softball while he lived with them. Zach eventually felt the time was right to go back to school and he received his teaching degree.

Chapter 17: Mending Old Wounds

"Come now, let us settle the matter," says the Lord. 'Though your sins are like scarlet, they shall be as white as snow; though they are red as crimson, they shall be like wool.'" Isaiah 1:18

Harley and Steve were returning to Platte after a successful day of selling pies in Kimball, South Dakota. They'd been working together for eight years by this time. During the long ride home, the conversation turned serious and Steve began to talk to Harley, for the first time, about what his life had been like when he was homeless in Des Moines

"Steve," Harley interrupted him, "I'm glad you brought it up. I've wanted to talk to you about when you left Marlene — when I didn't know where you were. Why didn't you tell me you were hurting so much?"

"Dad, I tried, but you didn't hear me."

After a long pause, Harley took a sharp breath," I'm sorry, Steve. Please forgive me for not being more understanding, for not being able to really listen to you at the time."

"I do forgive you and I'm sorry I put you through all that, Dad. You didn't deserve it. Please forgive me."

"I forgive you, son," Harley pledged.

With those words, a sense of peace that surpassed all understanding washed over Steve. It was second only to the time he pledged to follow Christ while on a forklift back in Chester, Iowa. Both Harley and Steve felt from that moment on that their relationship as father and son had been fully restored.

Steve & Harley

Harley's convincing preaching skills translated quite nicely for pie sales. Harley's stellar salesmanship was getting recognized everywhere he went, and he began to get quite a reputation as he traveled from grocery store to grocery store giving out samples, sounding more like an auctioneer as he sputtered out in one breath: "You wanna try some of my wife's pie? She makes the best pie in the state of Iowa." (If Harley were in another state, then he'd substitute the name of that state). "It's the best pie you can ever get! I married the best woman. I wouldn't trade her for a million dollars! I can't find a better one or a better pie. You ought to try it! It's the best pie you'll ever get! You wanna piece? Just try it! It's great!"

Steve would watch his father in disbelief, thinking it was the worst, corniest sales pitch in the world. But Harley's old-timer approach would get most people to at least stop and listen to this little, ancient man speak so quickly. Most of them would grin at him because he conducted his presentation with so much zest and zeal. And there wasn't a single person who turned down taking a pie sample.

Harley wasn't a prude. However, despite his loud and sometimes abrasive manner, he prided himself on living as virtuously as any man could. He didn't smoke, drink or swear. But in a changing world, he was often ill-equipped at handling comments that he believed went against the Bible's teaching. One time when the Freys were sampling pies by the bakery at a Hy-Vee store in Omaha, Harley returned with the pies to the front of the store where Berneice, Steve and Marie were waiting. Harley's face was bright red.

"What's the matter, Harley?" Berneice asked.

"Oh, Mama. ... I-I can't tell you," Harley stammered.

"What in the world happened?" Berneice demanded.

Harley sighed, "I was over in the bakery and the young women working over there ..." his voice trailed off.

"What?" Berneice questioned. "What did the young women do?'

"They said, 'That pie is good, you old *stud* you!'"

Harley hung his head, mortified.

"It's okay, Harley," Berneice reassured him as she secretly smiled to herself. She had no doubt whatsoever that Harley has always been loyal to her throughout their long marriage.

Harley & Berneice Frey

A short time later, the foursome was returning to Platte after working the grocery store circuit in Des Moines, when Harley complained of feeling ill. "I need to go to the doctor," Harley stated with urgency from the back seat of the car.

"Can you wait until we get to Sioux Falls, Dad?" Steve asked.

"I think so," Harley asserted, his voice cracking.

The hair on the back of Steve's neck stood up. There was something in his father's tone that alarmed him. He pressed down on the accelerator of the old Lincoln. Within an hour, they were approaching Sioux Falls. Steve drove right up to the hospital emergency room. He jumped out of the car and the three of them helped Harley, who had become extremely weak, into the ER. A nurse ushered the family into the waiting room, where they sat silently while doctors checked him out. Three hours later, a doctor wearing scrubs came out into the waiting area and called for the Freys.

"I'm Doctor Larsen," he said, introducing himself. "I'm an oncologist here at the hospital. I have some bad news. Please sit down," Dr. Larsen requested with gentleness, as he looked at Berneice. Steve and Marie held onto each other's hands as they lowered themselves in the waiting room chairs next to Berneice. Dr. Larsen took the seat on the other side of Berneice.

"You husband has cancer. It has spread throughout his entire body," Dr. Larsen announced.

Berneice gasped and put her hand to her mouth.

"What? How can that be? He was just fine. We were working, on our way back from Des Moines, and he was okay," Berneice shrieked.

"I'm sorry, it's a kind of cancer that if not detected early, well. ... There's really no way to stop it. There aren't any specific symptoms. Your husband and father has invasive melanoma. Unfortunately, it's very aggressive and has metastasized into many of his organs," Dr. Larsen explained, glancing at Steve. "We believe he has approximately two months to live."

Berneice hung her head and began to weep

uncontrollably. Steve and Marie looked at each other in disbelief. *How could this happen to the larger-than-life Harley?* They were unable to come to terms with the news that Harley was now suddenly dying.

"There's not much we can do for your father right now," Dr. Larsen continued. "We will set up an appointment to discuss the best possible course of action next week. But we will release him from the hospital in a few hours."

It was getting late, so Marie left to go get a couple of hotel rooms for the night, and called Ruth and Chuck and told them to come to Sioux Falls. Steve and Berneice stayed at the hospital to wait for Harley. Marie made it back to pick them up, just as Harley was being let out. They drove Harley over to the hotel, where Ruth and Chuck were waiting. Steve helped Harley into his room and as he lowered him into a chair, all the members of the family gathered around him.

"What's going on?" Harley questioned. "Is it that bad? You all look like you're going to my funeral," he barked, as he scanned their long faces.

"Yes, Dad," Steve gulped. "It is that bad. You're going to die."

"Well, I know I'm going to die!" Harley said, practically shouted. "Everyone is going to die! How soon are we talking about?"

Steve choked out the words, "You have two months."

Harley turned to look at Berneice, "Oh, Mama," he gasped, "That ain't very long, is it?"

Berneice, who had been trying to remain stoic, burst into tears, and she and Harley hugged one another, holding on tightly. Ruth and Chuck retreated to their own room, and Steve sat down on the bed in front of his parents.

"Dad," he sobbed, tears streaming down his face, "I would like to have one day with you — one uninterrupted day— that we can spend together, doing whatever you want, just you and me."

"Of course, son. We will do that," Harley promised. "But there's one thing I'd like. You're quite the woodworker, Steve. I'd like you to build my casket from scratch. Just a simple wooden casket is all I want. I don't want to take anything materialistic out of this world" he continued, "and let it be a sign of forgiveness between us."

"Yes, Dad, of course. It will by my honor and tribute to you," Steve uttered, as he worked to hold back his tears.

The family returned to Platte and continued to bake pies and deliver them throughout the region. Steve and Harley had more than one day to spend together, just talking and enjoying one another. But within a few weeks, the Platte Hospital admitted Harley as he grew weaker and weaker. Steve would complete parts of his casket and bring them up to the hospital for his dad to see and approve. He even ordered a pillow through the local funeral home and brought it up to his hospital room for Harley to try out. Harley placed the satin pillow behind his head.

"Yep, this is just fine, son. I can lay on this for eternity," Harley affirmed.

Harley remained in the Platte hospital for nearly a month, getting sicker by the day. He would sleep through some days entirely, but all the while his family kept a vigil by his side. Diane and Janice had returned to Platte, as well, and were staying with Steve and Marie.

As it became apparent that Harley did not have much longer to live, Steve went to the hospital every day that he could. One evening, in his weakened state, Harley took Steve's hand. Steve was immediately struck by the softness and gentleness of his father's hand. Harley's voice trembled as he confided, "Steve, I wish I could have been a better father to you."

"No, *no*, Dad," Steve choked. "I wish I could have been a better son!"

Still holding his father's hand, Steve bent over and Harley kissed him on the cheek. And Steve kissed his father back. As he stood up to leave, Steve noticed the minister of their church standing behind him and realized he must have witnessed the whole exchange.

The following day Steve made the drive to Waterloo, Iowa to promote *Grandma Frey's Homemade Pies* in the Hy-Vee stores there. That night, he received the call that his father had died peacefully. And while the news rocked Steve to his core, he knew in his heart that he and his father had reconciled completely and that his father *had* loved him. And despite all their ups and downs and Steve's journey down his broken road, Harley knew that his son loved him.

Harley's body was placed into the wooden casket that Steve had built, and it was taken in the Bethel Lutheran Church in Platte, where people travelled from all over the region to pay their respects. When the funeral was held, the church was jam-packed. The crowd even spilled out onto the front steps and sidewalks. Huge bouquets of flowers were crammed into every open area in the church.

His obituary in the local paper read: "Frey known for pies, cold ice cream, warm personality." Harley Frey was 73. The *Mitchell Daily Republic* article's lead line in the tribute to his life was that Harley had started his "thriving pie and ice cream business with a mere $50." It went on to quote Steve, who told the reporter, "I'll never live up to be as great of a man as my dad. He left a legacy I just can't fill."

Following the service, Harley's casket was loaded into a pickup truck with a topper on it. The family drove his body back to West Union, Iowa, where a second funeral service was held, just as packed as the first one. Harley had touched so many lives, from the pulpit as well as through the family business, and never had it been more evident than by the attendance at both of his funerals. Harley Frey was laid to rest in the Frey family plot in West Union.

Steve's reconciliation with his father and their final years together made him realize that another chapter in his life was needed to heal his brokenness and bring him closer to Christ and his own salvation.

Chapter 18: A House Divided
"If a house is divided against itself, it cannot stand."
Mark 3:25

In spite of Harley's death, *Grandma Frey's Homemade Pies* flourished. For seven years the business continued to grow. The pies made in Platte were available in 15 states. For the last couple of years, Steve and Marie spent most of their time on the road, going city-to-city and state-to-state to increase the number of stores that carried their pies.

While promoting their pies in Kansas City, Steve met George Frank Junior, a regular good ol' country boy, who was farm-raised and fattened. George was working as the frozen-food manager in a Hen House grocery store when one afternoon Steve approached him about putting *Grandma Frey's Homemade Pies* in his freezer cases.

"I'm Steve Frey," Steve said, introducing himself as he pumped George's big hand and forearm up and down.

"George Frank Junior," George drawled. "How can I help you, sir?"

"You look like the kind of guy who would like a blackberry pie! I'd like you to try my mother's recipe! I guarantee it will be *the* best blackberry pie you've ever tasted!" Steve promised.

"Humph," George scoffed. "I guarantee you don't have anything in your frozen pies that's as good as the ones my auntie made on the farm growing up. I picked the berries myself, and she baked up those pies as fast as she could.

Mmmmm," George said. His voice trailed off as he licked his lips at the memory of his auntie's homemade blackberry pies.

"I do believe you are wrong! My pie right here is just as close to your aunt's, if not better! I'll tell you what. Try *Grandma Frey's,* and if it's as good as your aunt's you have to buy a case of my pies to sell in your store," Steve challenged.

Convinced that no one could come close to his beloved auntie's recipe, George accepted Steve's proposition, and Steve eagerly dished him up a generous helping of blackberry pie. The minute George brought the fork to his mouth and began to taste *Grandma Frey's,* the look on his face gave it all away. It *was* as good as his dear aunt's pie. He couldn't believe it! *A frozen pie as good as homemade?* George didn't think that was even possible until this very moment.

"Ya' got me!" George acquiesced. "I guess I'm buying a case of pies."

"That's fantastic!" Steve said, thumping George on the back.

From that day on, the two men became fast friends, and George bought many a case of pies from Steve. A year later, George was feeling frustrated after being passed over for promotions in the store where he worked and he decided to call up Steve for some advice. A few moments into the conversation, Steve and Marie offered George a job as an account manager with Aristo Industries, servicing the grocery stores and restaurants that carried *Grandma Frey's Homemade Pies* in the Kansas City area. George immediately took them up on their offer.

George traveled up and down Interstate 35 from the northern Missouri state line all the way to the southern border and along Interstate 70 toward St. Louis. He was able to increase the number of accounts in the years he worked for Aristo in the Kansas City area and beyond from a little more than 60 to well over 300. During that time, the Freys also had to contract out with another company to make their pies in the area to meet the demand.

George spent months on the road, only seeing his wife and two young children on the occasional weekend when he could make it home. One Christmas Eve, Steve told George, "Now George, you've been working your butt off for us. I want you to go home this afternoon, and I don't want you to even think about work until after the New Year!"

"Alright," George agreed. "Heather will appreciate that. She's been feeling pretty alone lately with me on the road so much and with the kids to take care of."

"Then get yourself home and take care of your family!" Steve ordered.

George had a nice, quiet Christmas with his wife and children, but a few days after Christmas he began getting restless and decided he'd go down to the cold storage facility for the pies and check on the inventory. It wasn't more than 15 minutes after he'd left home that the phone rang and Heather answered.

"Where's George?" Steve asked on the other end of the line.

George had told Heather about Steve's orders, so she tried not give her husband away.

"He's not home right now," Heather answered.

"Well, where is he? He didn't go down to the warehouse, did he? I told him not to do that! He needs to spend time with you and the kids!"

"Well, Steve, he might have," Heather said.

And with that, Steve thanked her and hung up. Moments later he had the warehouse manager on the line.

"If you see George come in, have him call me right away," Steve told the manager.

George had just walked in the door as the facility manager was hanging up the phone. He knew he had to call Steve back, but he wasn't sure what to expect.

"George," Steve said after picking up the phone, "I gave you direct orders — you were not to work until after New Year's Day! What are you doing, man? Family has to be your first priority!"

"Uh, uh…" George stammered, "I just thought I should check and make sure everything was okay with the product."

"I've got people in the warehouse who can do that,

George! Now you go back home to your family and I don't want to catch you working again until after the New Year!"

"Okay, okay," George agreed, "You got it, boss!"

A few years later, all of the traveling that George had to do working for Aristo Industries began to take a real toll on his family. He called Steve to tell him he was going to look for a new job that didn't require travel. Instead of getting upset, Steve encouraged George and even wrote him a letter of recommendation that got him his next job. The two would remain life-long friends. George would often seek out Steve for advice on his career and family over the years.

* * *

Meanwhile, not all was idyllic between Steve and Marie, and Ruth and Chuck. The Anholts ran the company from Platte while the Freys were on the road. While Berneice helped out with the production of the pies, she had basically retired by this point. Growing up, Steve was considerably older than Ruth; he'd had a much closer relationship with his other two sisters.

Ruth and Chuck followed Harley and Berneice to Platte, and she convinced Harley to let her open the restaurant. While the restaurant venture hadn't gone well, Steve had helped the family ice cream and pie business flourish. When it came right down to it, Ruth resented him for it. Harley had always held the family together, but now that he was gone, Ruth's animosity toward Steve and Marie was much more overt. And Chuck was a hothead. He'd felt passed up by Harley, once Steve helped form the company and gained his father's favor.

Chuck, as president of Aristo Industries, and Ruth, as treasurer, had control over the finances of the company and because they were family, Steve and Marie never really questioned them about the money. However there was an incident that would later be an indicator of what was to come. One of their suppliers contacted Marie to say he hadn't been paid. Marie told him she thought that was odd, and he said that payments from Aristo Industries kept coming later and later.

So this time, when none showed up at all, he really wasn't surprised. When Marie questioned Ruth about it, she told her there must have been some kind of mistake, that the bill just was overlooked. Ruth reassured Marie that it would be paid immediately.

Steve and Marie had just spent three weeks working in Kansas City, where *Grandma Frey's* were stocked in several stores. Upon their return home to Platte, they were greeted by a local sheriff's deputy, who was sitting in his car in their driveway. When he saw them pulled in, he got out of his car and approached them. He handed them papers and rigidly announced, "You've been served."

Steve and Marie look at each other, bewildered. They both assumed it had something to do with the business; maybe it was from an angry competitor threatening them with a lawsuit. They went inside their house and opened the envelope and couldn't believe what was inside. Ruth and Chuck were demanding they get out of the business and turn it over to them!

"Wiener, what in the world?" Marie said. She was astonished.

"I don't know, Marie," Steve answered, shaking his head. But we are getting them on the phone, and we're going to ask to meet them at the office.

Thirty-minutes later, the two couples were standing across from one another in the office in the old bank building on Main Street.

"Ruth," Steve addressed his sister. "What in the world is going on? We don't understand."

"Steve, we just want you and Marie out. I started this business with Mom and Dad in the café, and now Chuck and I want to run it by ourselves," Ruth said with a steely determination.

"*We* want control of the company," Chuck angrily pronounced.

"Chuck, you're already president of Aristo Industries. Isn't that enough?" Steve asked.

Years ago, they had determined that Chuck would be

president, Steve the vice president, Ruth the treasurer, and Marie the secretary.

"No, Steve, it's not. Ruth and I have decided that this is what we want, and if you want to fight us, we'll see you in court! Don't forget, my dad is on the board of our company, so we have you outnumbered!"

And with that, Ruth and Chuck stormed out of the office, leaving Marie and Steve with stunned looks on their faces.

"They gave us no real explanation," Marie said incredulously to Steve.

As they turned to leave, Steve looked at Marie and said, "We should have seen this coming, Marie. They've always resented us coming in and changing direction. This is the death of our company."

A few days later, Ruth, Chuck and Chuck's father voted Steve and Marie out as vice president and secretary of the company. Ruth and Chuck asked Steve and Marie to meet again and offered them $10,000 to walk away from the business. But their answer was a resounding, "no!" They told Steve and Marie that if they wouldn't quit, they might as well continue with the sales of the pies. At that point, Steve and Marie actually wanted to leave. But they also felt the pull of obligation toward their company shareholders and their suppliers who preferred to deal with them rather than Ruth or Chuck.

His sister's betrayal hit Steve hard and he fell into a depression. Both he and Marie felt as if everything they'd worked so hard for, what Harley and Berneice had helped build, was about to fail. Steve prayed and prayed, but the situation seemed hopeless. The only ones benefiting from this family fight were the lawyers Steve and Ruth had each hired.

Steve was driving on Highway 50 from Avon to Platte one day, feeling overwhelmed by the untenable situation. He pulled over to pray aloud:-"Jesus, I need some direction. Do you want me to continue doing this? I've done everything possible to try to make this right, but I'm failing. Help me, Lord, I need a sign."

With those words, Steve pulled back onto the highway. Something seemed to draw him to the next farmhouse that he saw. It was almost as if the car was driving itself. Before he knew it, he was in the driveway. Then, for some reason, he thought he should give this family a pie, so he pulled up to the door, got out of his car and went around to his trunk and grabbed an apple pie. Then he went to the door, not knowing why he was there. He just had an overwhelming sense that he was supposed to be there.

Steve knocked and was greeted by a woman as she opened the door.

"Hello, ma'am. I'm Steve Frey from Platte."

"Oh," a look of recognition spread across the woman's face. "I know who you are! You're the man from Platte with the pie company!"

"Yes, ma'am, I am."

"Won't you please come in," the woman motioned for him to step inside the doorway. She was a pleasant-looking Midwestern farm wife, slightly plump with brown, wavy hair and glasses. He stepped inside the door.

"I'm Anne Adamson," she said, introducing herself.

"Pleased to meet you, Anne! Won't you please have this pie, on me," Steve bowed slightly.

"Why thank you so much!" she exclaimed. "Can you please wait here a minute?" Anne quickly vanished into another room and reappeared a few seconds later with a man at her side who was tall and wiry. He had black hair and brown eyes and the leathery skin of a farmer who'd worked years in the fields. "This is my husband, John," she said to Steve.

"Pleased to meet you, John," Steve said as he stuck out his hand in greeting. The two men shook hands and began to talk. There was something about this man's presence that compelled Steve to open up to him. He told him how he had been born again in Christ after dedicating his life to him. John nodded in understanding.

"Yes, I've heard about you," John said, and then he excused himself, saying, "I believe I have something for you."

Steve wondered what in the world this stranger could have for him. It didn't take long for him to return to the living room where the two men had been talking. John held an envelope in his hands. He pushed it into Steve's hand.

"I'd like to invest in your company," John affirmed.

Steve opened the envelope. It contained several thousand dollars. Steve couldn't believe it.

"What? Why?" Steve asked, astounded.

"The Lord had been good to us," John began, "and I've been asking him what I should do with this extra money. Where should I invest it? And then you show up at my door. And something inside of me just said *this is it! This is where you should invest your money, with his man.* I know that voice and I know to obey it."

Steve's jaw nearly dropped to the floor. As he regained his composure he said, "Thank you, from the bottom of my heart, John. You have no idea what this means to me, especially right now. I'll draw up the paperwork to make you an official investor in Aristo Industries!" Steve exclaimed.

Tears welled up in Steve's eyes, and the two men continued to talk about the business while Anne served the apple pie, complete with ice cream on top. Then Steve told the couple he needed to get back on the road.

"I'm so glad I stopped by here," Steve told them. "You've provided me with a real miracle and renewed my faith"

Steve drove away from the farmhouse two hours after he first arrived. He turned back onto the highway in the direction he'd come from, opposite of home. He drove back to the spot where he had prayed to Jesus for direction and turned off the engine.

"Thank you, Jesus!" Steve proclaimed aloud. "I will be faithful. I will not lose hope." The irony of the fact that he had prayed so many times over the years while pulled over on the side of the road, and that his prayers had been answered, wasn't lost on him. With that, he drove the 30 miles back home to Platte. Upon arriving, he called up his attorney, who advised him just to hold onto John's money for now.

"It's all coming to a head," his attorney told him. "Whatever you do, don't turn that money over to Ruth and Chuck. They are just about out of money, and they won't be able to keep the business running much longer. "

The legal battle and hatred that Steve felt from his sister and her husband intensified. Even though John Adamson's money was safely sitting in a separate bank account, Steve couldn't see an end in sight or know if he'd ever be able to use it at all. He lay awake and night and cried. Marie tried to console him, but her attempts were useless. Steve couldn't stop thinking about how he and his father had started Aristo Industries with such high hopes. Steve felt like a failure because he couldn't keep it going at the same level that he and Harley had, while Harley was alive. Somehow, the fact that his sister had turned on him seemed like a reflection of his own weakness. Marie and Steve had even begun to fear for their own safety. They got up and worked every day, but a dark cloud followed them everywhere they went.

On one of his trips to a grocery store in White Lake, Steve pulled over to pray once again. He remembered back to the time when he had pulled that old Pontiac over while it was on fire and sat by the wheel and prayed. The car had miraculously started up again. He thought about the prayers on the side of the road just a few months ago, before John Adamson offered his financial support and interest in the company. He thanked Jesus for being so faithful, even while he doubted his future and the Lord's plans for him. He whispered his prayers of thanks and then begged for another sign to keep pushing forward. As he finished his prayer, he looked up and there before him was another farm house.

Steve pulled up in the gravel driveway and got out of his car. Once again, a woman answered the door and he introduced himself.

"Of course!" she affirmed, as if she'd been expecting him. "I know who you are! Please come in."

Then she turned and called out the back door, "Russell, please come in. We've got company!"

A man of about 65 came into the house. He had a thick head of gray-black hair and liquid blue eyes.

"I'm Steve Frey," Steve said to the farmer. "I'm a Christian man. I'm just out meeting the public, representing our company and I'd like to give you a pie."

"I'm Russell Moore," he said, "And that's fantastic. Thank you so much."

Steve went on to tell him a little bit about how he and his father had started Aristo Industries and how *Grandma Frey's Homemade Pies* were in so many grocery stores in many states now. While he was talking, Russell interrupted him:

"Steve, farming has been very good to me. Would it be possible for me to be involved in your company? I've got some money. I'd like to invest if you'd let me."

And with that, Russell walked over to open a drawer in the kitchen and took out his checkbook. He scribbled on the check and then ripped it out of the pad and turned to show it to Steve. Steve took a sharp inhale upon reading the amount. Steve asked Russell to pray with him and the two men bowed their heads as they sat at the kitchen table, giving glory to God. As Steve turned to leave, Russell called out to him, "Steve, if you ever need any help, my son is high up in state government."

"Thanks, Russell. I'll let you know."

But Steve never had to call on Russell's son. A few days later, through their attorney, Ruth and Chuck demanded that Steve turn over the money he had raised from the two farmers. But on his attorney's advice, Steve told them he would not give them the money. It turned out that Ruth and Chuck only had enough money left to keep the business in operation for five more days. In a conference call with the attorneys, Chuck said, "We will turn over the company to you and give you our stock shares, if you give us Marie's Mazda Miata."

Steve and Marie looked at each other in disbelief. Marie has splurged on the little red sports car in 1990 and babied it. It was only worth about $7,000. However, the stock shares weren't really worth anything now. Before Steve could say anything, Marie jumped in:

"Of course," she agreed, without hesitation. "It's yours. You can have it!"

A few days later, Marie had the title to the car put in Ruth's and Chuck's names, and she wrote a note and placed it on the windshield, which read:

We love you Ruth & Chuck. We hope you enjoy this car as much as we did!

Ruth and Chuck did not respond to that note and a short time later packed up all their belongings in the middle of the night and moved to Thief River Falls, Minnesota, where Janice was living. A short time later, the couple declared bankruptcy and refused to pay off any of the debts they had left behind in Platte.

Berneice, who had long ago sided with Ruth, went with them. Ruth had power of attorney over Berneice and had filled Berneice's head with all kinds of stories about Steve and Marie that had altered Berneice's opinion of them. Although Steve has sent letters to Ruth and Chuck, seeking reconciliation, neither Ruth nor Chuck has spoken to Steve or Marie since.

Berneice had been complaining of backaches and was diagnosed with cancer. She ended up living with Janice because the eldest Frey daughter was a trained nurse. A month later, Janice placed a call to Steve. "Mom is asking for you, Steve. You need to come now," Janice said, her voice cracking with emotion over the line.

"Marie and I will be there as soon as we can," Steve promised.

A short time later, Steve and Marie were on the road, making the seven-hour drive to northwestern Minnesota. They arrived at Janice's house in the early evening. Janice ushered them in and took Steve into a back bedroom where Berneice lay in pain on the bed. The cancer had spread to her bones and she was on a strong dose of morphine. Steve looked at his mother, who seemed just a shadow of herself, and as if she were a million miles away.

"Hi, Mom," Steve uttered softly. "I'm here, Mom. It's your son, Steve. I love you, Mom." Steve's eyes welled up with tears.

But Berneice did not acknowledge Steve. While her eyes were open, she offered no response to his words. Steve hung his head and began to weep. Then Berneice turned to Janice and asked for a blanket. Steve realized, as he began to back out of the room, that this would be the last time he would ever see his mother alive. She was departing this earth without being reconciled to her son: something Steve would have to live with for the rest of his days.

Steve and Marie headed back to Platte. To Steve, the road before them seemed to never end. Steve was grieving for his mother and for himself and for the loss of any chance of reconciliation. Marie, who was driving, looked over at him with empathy and compassion. "Would you like to pray about it, Wiener?"

Steve nodded his head in agreement, as silent tears began to stream down his cheeks. "Dear Lord," Steve began. "Please forgive me for letting my mother down so many times. I forgive her for holding onto her hard feelings so tightly. Please be there to greet her in heaven and let us meet once again in the love and peace of Heaven. Thank you for my mother's love and guidance."

With those words, Steve felt a wave of calm wash over him. Even though seeing his mother for the last time didn't turn out the way he would have liked or how it often does in the movies — with a tearful reconciliation and final words spoken of love and acceptance — he now felt as if things were okay anyway. He could go on with his life, without being wracked with guilt and shame. He had done his part. He had shown up and he had told her he loved her. That was all God wanted of him.

Steve had been back in Platte for a couple of days after that unfulfilling visit with his mother when the phone rang. "Steve, this is Pastor Egstad. Would you please come over to the church tonight at 7:30?" Pastor Carl Egstad asked.

Steve agreed and hung up the phone. But he wondered what it could be about. *Was he going to be chided for the fallout with his sister and brother-in-law?*

But that night when he arrived at Bethel Lutheran Church, he saw through the window Pastor Egstad and four board members inside. He saw a table set with a white tablecloth. Placed on top were the communion dishes and lit candles. As he walked in, one by one, each man embraced him and then they brought him over to the table.

"Steve," Pastor Egstad began, "We know the pressures you've been under lately with the break with your sister and her husband, and now with your mother on her deathbed. We just want to have communion with you and tell you that we love you."

The men sat around the table and took part in communion together. Then they joined hands and prayed for Steve. Steve felt his heart heal in those moments, and his spirits soared.

Berneice died a few days later. Berneice's funeral was held at Bethel Lutheran in Platte and her body was buried in West Union next to Harley's.

Chapter 19: Forging Ahead

"The righteous shall move onward and forward; those with pure hearts shall become stronger and stronger." Job 17:9

The year was 2007; four years after Ruth and Chuck left the family business. Steve and Marie worked tirelessly at the pie company. They vowed to pay off all of Ruth's and Chuck's debts, but even with the funds of their generous investors, it was a daunting task. In one 24-hour period, they would sometimes swing through three states, covering hundreds of miles and stop in dozens of grocery stores. It was after returning home from one of these exhausting trips that Steve approached Marie.

"Marie," he began. "I can't do this anymore. I'm tired and I know you are, too. I believe it's time to sell the company."

Marie nodded and then asked, "Who will you ask to buy it?"

"I'm not sure, but the first offer I get, I'm taking it."

A few days later, Steve made the trip to Madison, Wisconsin for a meeting with the chief executive officer of Dawn's Foods. The food-production company had started off making potato salad and was now offering 85 different products carried in grocery stores throughout the Midwest.

"I'm here to sell *Grandma Frey's Homemade Pies*!" Steve announced to a room full of executives. "I plan to accept the first offer I get. After our meeting, I'm headed to Des Moines to meet with the executives of Hy-Vee stores."

Then Steve named his price. The Dawn's Foods executives asked him to step out of the office so they could talk it over.

Ten minutes later, a secretary motioned for him to return.

"You've got it!" the CEO affirmed.

Steve couldn't believe that the first company he approached was willing to meet his price. It couldn't be this easy, but in fact, it was. On a handshake, Dawn's Foods bought Aristo Industries' recipes, Berneice's picture and the trademark. *Grandma Frey's Homemade Pies* would continue on without the Frey family.

Steve used what he could of proceeds of the sales to make things right with his investors. But other people Ruth and Chuck had owed money, like Tom Nielsen, an auto mechanic in Platte who had done work on their personal vehicles as well as the Aristo delivery trucks, remained unpaid.

Marie took a job working as a cashier at the Casey's convenience store. Steve started a farmer's market in the old bank building where the pies had been produced. He ran the market for a few seasons, but then sold the building to an antiques dealer, who planned to open a store in the old Aristo Industries location. Steve didn't like just sitting around the house while Marie worked at Casey's; Marie wasn't much fond of it either. So when a one-story, 11-foot by 20-foot, little brick garage at the end of a row of shops became available on Main Street in Platte, Steve jumped at the chance to rent it. Steve was going back to what he knew best — serving up helpings of the rich Aristo ice cream recipe, topped with sprinkles of love. *Little Brick Ice Cream* was born.

But the empty garage was far from ready to serve customers. There wasn't even a door on the back end. It had been the garage for an apartment upstairs. There was no electricity. But rent was dirt-cheap, and Steve knew he could transform the place into what he envisioned. Steve did all the wiring, put in a tile floor, and nailed sheet rock to the walls. While he worked on the building, he remembered the time when he was young and had helped Harley finish the basement in their home. He realized his father had taught him so much and he silently thanked him for it.

They Freys already had the ice cream dipping cabinets, ice cream machine and other equipment from their former business. A few weeks later they were ready for customers.

"Let's call it *Little Brick,*" Marie suggested one night, "After all, it's in a little brick building and I think it's kind of catchy!"

"Sounds good to me!" Steve agreed, nodding.

The small building held the ice cream counter, and when people wanted to come in and sit down, the Freys had set up some milk crates in the back of the room. On the walls, Steve and Marie hung *Aristo Ice Cream* and *Grandma Frey's Homemade Pies* memorabilia. Marie made 80 different flavors of ice cream, rotating the various favors on different weeks. She worked late into the night to make the ice cream, still spending her days managing the Casey's. She churned out the vanilla ice cream and then added licorice, Snickers, fudge, Oreos and Butterfingers to create flavors. Marie named one of her flavors "Kiss My Grass," where she churned in mint, toasted coconut and Hershey Kisses. Adults gravitated toward her Coffee Crunch and kids often ordered Purple Cow, which was grape flavored. The Freys charged $2 for a cone or cup. For children, it was just 50 cents.

Little Brick Ice Cream began to gain quite the reputation across several counties. People came from miles away just to sample the frozen treat. Steve and Marie decided to expand from ice cream to food and began serving spaghetti and meatballs, turkey with mashed potatoes and gravy, broasted chicken and walking tacos. The food was served buffet style — "all you can eat" for just $5. Before long, it was evidence that the little, 11-foot-by-20-foot space wasn't enough room. The main floor next door was also empty, so Steve was able to rent that and began the process of remodeling it. They found some restaurant booths someone was getting ready to throw away and refurbished them. The man who owned the local lumberyard made them some tables, and they collected chairs from various sales. Within a few months they were ready to open seating for 40 people. He also told the mechanic, Tom Nielsen, that while he may not be able to pay off Ruth's and Chuck's debts to him, he and his wife could eat at his restaurant for free.

Steve opened for lunch from 11 a.m. to 1 p.m. every day.

It didn't take long for the high school students in Platte, who were allowed to go home for lunch, to discover *Little Brick*. For $5, they filled up on all they could eat and enjoyed the company of its goofy proprietor. Steve had hung a guitar on the wall and when the kids were in his restaurant he would take it down and sing a tune, badly out of key. The students laughed and often joined in. Steve, always dressed in bib overalls, prided himself on running one of the friendliest businesses in town.

One of *Little Brick's* first customers was a man who Steve knew from his days in the old bank building from running the pie business. Brian Balster had operated a manufacturing business few doors down. The two men had exchanged pleasantries and occasionally had borrowed various pieces of equipment from one another, or had lent each other a helping hand from time to time.

Brian had come in to order chicken and ice cream one day, and the two men struck up a conversation. Only this time that conversation was deeper than any other they'd had over the years. They realized they both shared a strong Christian faith that they felt compelled to act upon. Brian had his own story, and while it was different than Steve's, they'd both experienced low points in their lives that had brought them close to Christ. Both and been broken by the world and circumstances and both had found healing in God's love. Now Brian and Steve had hearts on fire to do the Lord's bidding.

Brian saw clearly that while on the outside, Steve appeared to be a fun-loving, often wacky man who loved to joke and kid around, inside his heart was open and raw, and that he truly desired that everyone he meet come to know the Jesus he knew, the One who had saved his life.

The two struck up a fast friendship, and on any given morning at the *Little Brick* in Platte you can still find Brian and Steve and possibly another friend or two sharing coffee and engaging in prayer. The men are determined to live out their faith, which means more than going to church and doing the right thing. Every day with tears in his eyes Steve asks, *"Whom can I speak to today, Lord? Who can I help? What can I do to bring glory to Your name?"* The men believe that Jesus is right there with them at that table in *Little Brick* and symbolically leave an empty chair for Him to sit beside them. For Jesus is not just a nice idea, but rather a real, living being in their eyes. And the proof is in their own lives and how He transformed them.

Chapter 20: The Big Fish Story

"And He said unto them, "Follow Me, and I will make you fishers of men." Matthew 4:19

Steve's oldest daughter, Hannah, had met her future husband, Roger Vandenbos, in Platte while she was visiting Marie and Steve. Roger worked at a nearby commercial hog farm and they had settled into a home in Platte and had three children. Hannah was a stay-at-home mom, but during the summer of 2013, Hannah was struggling with depression and decided she didn't want to be married to Roger any longer. One evening, Steve and Marie got a desperate call from Roger, telling them that Hannah had threatened to take her own life. He had rushed Hannah over to Pastor Joel Davis' home for guidance.

Steve and Marie arrived, nearly out of breath at Pastor Davis' door. His wife ushered them inside and they found Hannah in a back room, lying on the couch. The minister and his wife, and Steve and Marie surrounded Hannah and told her how much they all loved her. Then Marie said to Hannah: "We need to get you some help, Hannah. Will you agree to get help?"

Hannah nodded. Then Steve asked, "What can I do for you, Hannah?"

Hannah looked imploringly at Steve, "Please leave, Dad. I'd like you and Marie to leave now."

"Only if you promise to get help," Steve begged.

"I promise, Dad," Hannah assured him. "I will."

"Okay then, Marie and I will leave. But you need to know that we love you dearly," Steve said, looking at Hannah with compassion. He understood exactly how his daughter felt. It seemed like a lifetime ago now, but he, too, had been in that very dark place and knew exactly how hopeless Hannah must be.

Pastor Davis and his wife arranged for Hannah to meet with a counselor the next day. Two days later, on June 10, Steve and Marie had invited anyone in the community who had caught fish over at the Missouri River or one of the nearby lakes, to come in for a fish fry. They had a packed and boisterous house. But just as everyone was sitting down for the feast, Roger came running into the restaurant,

"Hannah's gone!" he proclaimed in a panicked voice. "Hannah's gone!" Roger repeated.

The fish fry quickly came to an end, and Steve and Marie got in their car to go look for Hannah and the kids. When they couldn't find them anywhere in town, they called police. But even law enforcement was unable to locate them.

Months later, Steve and Marie would learn that Hannah had left with the couple's three children and taken them out of state. Her mother, Marlene, who still lived in Colorado, had met Hannah halfway and brought them to her house. The irony of the fact that his daughter had left Roger much in the same way he had left Marlene was not lost upon Steve. While she had not left her children as he had, he now understood exactly what his dad must have felt when he learned that Steve was gone, all those years ago in West Union. Steve felt nothing but compassion for Hannah, but as much as he had been the prodigal son, wanting nothing to do with his family during those low points in his life, Hannah now wanted nothing to do with him.

Steve spent many nights crying over Hannah's departure, unable to come to terms that his daughter had left. He and Marie both had enjoyed living close to them and being able to spend time with their grandchildren. Now all that had come to an end, and there was no real explanation from Hannah about why. But Steve knew that *he* never really had a good reason for his behavior when he left Marlene, at least not anything that reasonable people would understand.

Steve found himself deeply depressed once again in his life. His typical jovial nature was gone, replaced with a deep sadness. He had a difficult time even going into *Little Brick*, let alone interacting with his customers. One night Marie told him he needed to do something, anything, to get out of his funk.

"I just want to sell the place," he said, sobbing.

"Okay. We will sell it," Marie agreed.

It turned out there was an interested buyer, and the Freys had no trouble selling *Little Brick*. A couple of young women agreed to run the restaurant and wanted to change its name. But they were not interested in keeping the ice cream shop going. For the next two month, Steve barely left home. He sank deeper and deeper into a black abyss of which there seemed to be no way out. He tried to pray, but he stood alone feeling isolated in God's silence.

One evening after returning home from Casey's, Marie told him, "You've got do something! I love you too much to just sit back and watch you suffer like this. You can't change what's happened with Hannah. But you must have some other purpose in your life, Wiener," she demanded, not unkindly.

"You're right," Steve acquiesced. "I must do something. I just don't know what."

While someone else was running their former restaurant, the entrepreneur in Steve knew that another businesses must be out there for him. He and Marie learned there was an empty building available to rent a few doors down from their last business on Main Street. Steve decided to open a candy store, believing that interacting with the children in town could be just what he needed to get out of his funk. Soon customers were coming in the doors, asking for the famous Aristo ice cream. Marie figured this would be the best way to bring the Steve she had come to love so much back to life again, and she agreed to start making it once more. The *Little Brick* was resurrected in a new location.

But Steve wasn't back to his old self again. As he struggled emotionally, he was filled with doubt. One evening after working in the shop, he knelt down to pray:

"God, I've never asked You for something specific like this before. But my daughter, Hannah, is gone and it's tearing my heart out — worse than anything I've ever experienced so far. This is my daughter. Do You even care? Do You even know I'm alive? I've given You 34 years of my life. I'm going out fishing tomorrow. I know it sounds stupid, Lord, but I want to catch the biggest fish I've ever caught. I need a sign that You're real God. If You're so powerful, please put that fish on my line."

The following day was a Monday and Steve drove out to Roosevelt Lake, a tributary of the Missouri River, hauling his small fishing boat behind his truck. Steve put the boat in his water and put a lure on his line and cast it into the water. Nearly immediately after casting the line, he felt a tug. His heart leaped as he pulled the line in. At the end of his line was probably the biggest largemouth bass he'd ever seen, certainly the biggest he'd ever caught. The bass was five pounds and nearly two feet long. Steve reeled it in, and put it at the bottom of his boat. He hurriedly steered the boat to shore and hitched it back up to his truck, and jumped in and drove back to Platte as fast as he could. He could barely contain his excitement. He pulled up in front of Casey's and grabbed the fish and stood outside the big window. He could see Marie behind the counter. He held up the fish, his heart nearly bursting with joy. Marie looked out from behind the counter and spotted him and burst out in laughter.

Steve took the fish home and placed it on the workbench in his garage. He went into the house and got down on his knees and began to utter prayers of thanksgiving: *"God, I hear You. I know You are real. Thank You for answering my prayers!"*

Steve's prayers became more fervent in the days that followed, and his faith grew. The deep despair that had enveloped him since Hannah left was dissipating. He felt called to go fishing again. So the following Monday, he hitched his trailer with his boat back up to his vehicle and headed back to the same spot where he had caught that big bass.

It was another hot summer day, the sun beating down on him, even though it wasn't even midday yet. Steve set the boat in the water and loaded up his rod and reel and tackle box. He put a worm on the hook and cast the line, saying a silent prayer to himself in praise of Jesus as he did so. It barely touched the water when he felt a tug. This was stronger than the last. He couldn't believe it. It was so heavy; it was a struggle for him to bring in the line. When he finally had the fish out of the water, he gasped out loud: *"Oh my Lord! God is good!"*

Another largemouth bass was at the end of his line. This was one was even bigger than the last at about six pounds and nearly three feet long. *The Lord does love me*, he thought to himself and then he uttered this prayer: *"Thank you, God, for never leaving my side, for being faithful, even when I had no faith."*

God's message came through to him with clarity he'd never known. Despite the pain, God was giving him more blessings than he could imagine. Never in his wildest dreams did he imagine catching such big bass in this little lake. He felt his faith restored once again.

He quickly drove this even-bigger fish back into Platte to show Marie.

Steve Frey with his two big fish

A few days later, Roger asked Steve to go fishing with him. "Okay," Steve agreed. "But get ready because God is teaching me a lesson!"

The following Monday was the third Monday that Steve went fishing that month. The two men headed over to Roosevelt Lake. The day was another steamer, but they were glad for one another's company. No sooner had they gotten the boat in the water and Steve cast his line when he felt a tug. He held on tight as the pole bent over into the water. "Roger, get the net! This one is unbelievable!"

Steve jumped to his feet as he struggled to pull in his catch. He could barely keep ahold of the pole.

"Roger, if you don't get it in the net, I'm throwing you in!" Steve threatened, jokingly.

Roger put the net in the water, and Steve guided the fish by the hook right into the net. He couldn't believe the size of it. It was giant of a Northern pike. He thought his last two fish were unbelievable. *Well, this was one for the record books*! They hauled the net over the edge of the boat and the fish landed at the bottom, flopping around so much that it nearly capsized the eight-foot long boat. The monster pike was 15 pounds and 36 inches long.

Steve couldn't wait to get back into town to show Marie this one. Roger and Steve drove over to the Casey's and Steve took the fish out of the back of the pickup. He held it up to the window. Marie couldn't believe the size of that fish. She grabbed her camera and left the register to take a picture of it.

"God gives you so much more than you can even ask for!" Steve proclaimed, as he grinned from ear to ear.

Steve's 15 pounder!

Steve didn't want to be greedy, but he figured God answered his prayers on those three Mondays in August, so he'd head back to Roosevelt Lake once again on the next Monday. This time he was alone. He sat in his boat, rod and reel in hand. But the fish just weren't biting. It was 85 degrees. Steve figured he'd pressed his luck this time and had asked for too much. Two hours passed and the sweat ran down Steve's temples and on the back of his neck. He set his pole down and spoke out loud to God: *"God, I haven't had a bite on my line today, but I know You have everything under control. I know that You love me. I know that You're talking to me. I know how powerful You are. I know if I needed a fish, I could cast out there and You would place a fish on my hook if it would save my life. I understand now how important I am to You. I know You can do it, I don't doubt You anymore!"*

With those words, not expecting anything, Steve picked up his fishing rod and cast his line out once again. The lure hit the water and out of the water leaped a fish; it had taken hold of the bait. Steve jumped up: *"That's from You God! I know now in my heart that Hannah is okay."*

But Steve got so excited that he lost the fish as he tried to reel it into the boat. It didn't matter. God had created these miracles in his life. And that was the day Steve's heart stopped crying for Hannah, for himself, for his failures, for his mother's rejection, his sister's betrayal. There was a message in God's fish story that he heard with his heart He told him: *Go in peace; all is well and proclaim My love to all who will listen.* He felt the completeness of God's love and from that day onward his faith never wavered, no matter his circumstances. It was as if God had finished writing the words on his heart to complete the love poem that He began when Steve jumped off that forklift in Chester, so many years ago.

Steve pledged to God that he would tell his "Big Fish Story" to all who would listen, and so he has. Just stop into the *Little Brick* sometime and ask him. He'll even show you the pictures!

Chapter 21: **Spreading His Word**

"Go therefore and make disciples of all the nations, baptizing them in the name of the Father and of the Son and of the Holy Spirit, teaching them to observe all things that I have commanded you; and lo, I am with you always, even to the end of the age." Matthew 28:19-20

When Steve lost that last fish, he knew that his daughter, Hannah's life was in God's hands and that he had to let her go and complete his own mission. All of his life experiences cumulated in that single moment in his boat out on Roosevelt Lake, and he felt renewed in spirit and in energy. He also noticed something quite peculiar. That insecurity — the empty hole that had practically consumed his entire life — was gone. Maybe it was a gradual process where he was healed by a greater love, but it seemed sudden to him. His inferiority complex has vanished and was replaced by confidence: a confidence in God's love and that he had a message to spread in His name.

Filled with the Holy Spirit, Steve knew what he had to do. It seemed as clear to him as that warm summer day, with its crystal blue skies and milky white clouds. He was going to reopen *Little Brick* in its original little brick building. The women who'd purchased the business a few months earlier had just told Marie that it wasn't going well. The thought popped into his head, like a sprout out of a seed: *He would buy it back!* He rushed over to the restaurant and spoke with the new owners and they immediately took him up on his offer. *Little Brick* was back in business!

The smell of broasted chicken and fried potato wedges filled the place just days later. Steve hung back up all of his Aristo Industries and *Grandma Frey's Homemade Pies* memorabilia, and within hours a steady stream of people began pouring in for lunch. Steve couldn't believe how easy it was. It seemed like a miracle that everything fell into place so quickly. Steve didn't know exactly how God was going to use him, but he knew he was supposed to be running this restaurant and ice cream counter. He knew he was supposed to share his Big Fish Story with everyone who walked through the door, not *just* about the fish, necessarily, but how Christ had saved his life and lightened his burdens.

And so it began. His life's mission was a ministry handed down by The Most High on a sweltering July day in the middle of Roosevelt Lake. If Steve had made different choices, he may have followed in his father's footsteps and become a preacher with his own church. But that wasn't in the cards for Steve now and he truly felt some regret over that. Instead, his pulpit would be behind the ice cream case, as he served up one of Marie's 50 flavors. He said a silent prayer, asking God for direction. Every morning when he woke, he prayed: *God, I am your servant, please show me what you want me to do today. Who can I help today?*

Not a week has passed that Steve wasn't able to touch someone's life who walked through the doors of *Little Brick.*

* * *

One day Steve received a letter from Hannah, who he had learned relocated just an hour away from Platte so that her children could visit their father. It was a letter he had anxiously searched the mailbox for every day for over the last 18 months. Steve's heart leapt for joy as he hurriedly ripped open the envelope. Only five words were written on the stationary:

Dad,
I love you,
Hannah

While it wasn't much, Steve took heart in the fact that it was a message of love, rather than hate. He quickly responded:

Hannah,
You are my first-born daughter. I love you, beyond a shadow of a doubt. I love you with all my heart. My house is your house. You are welcome here any time. I love you dearly,
Your father

But for six long months, Hannah's response was only silence. Then one day another letter from her did arrive. But this time, there was nothing personal in her words. It was as if someone else had composed it:

Dear Dad,
Just to bring you up-to-date on what your grandchildren are doing ...

Hannah went on to list what each child was involved with. But Steve already knew all that because he saw his grandchildren each time they visited Roger. And then she signed it:

Hannah

Not *Love, Hannah*, just Hannah. But Steve refused to be discouraged. He composed another letter to his daughter:

Hannah,
I told you before and I'll say it again: I love you deeply. You owe me nothing; no explanation; nothing. I love you and I always will. My house is your house. Please come home.
Love,
Your father.

Steve dropped the letter in the post box, full of hope that at least the line of communication with his daughter would remain open. But that was not to be. Steve has not heard from Hannah since. However, Steve counted his blessings that he remained close to his son-in-law, Roger, and had a good relationship with his grandchildren. Steve thought about how Harley had patiently waited for the return of his prodigal son and he would do no less for his prodigal daughter. Steve clung to the hope of her return into his life for however long it took.

* * *

There was no shortage of people coming into *Little Brick* needing encouragement, and even though there would always be something missing without Hannah in his life, Steve poured his heart into his vocation. And God didn't let him down.

Steve and Marie encountered three to four people *every week* who were seeking guidance, encouragement, support or just a shoulder to cry on.

One of them was Kim Kern. Kim and her husband, Jesse, along with her parents, Roger and Diane Jensen, kept a camper in the summer at the Platte Creek Recreation Area. Kim had met Marie while she worked behind the counter at Casey's convenience store. After just a few brief encounters, Kim felt as if she'd been friends with Marie her entire life. Marie invited Kim's family over to *Little Brick,* and it didn't take long before they were sitting down to chicken dinners. Steve and Kim's dad, Roger, hit it off immediately. Roger was a crude man who had worked in construction his whole life and had battled an alcohol addiction. It didn't take long for Steve to share his story with Roger and offer him hope and words of wisdom. As the summer progressed Steve and Marie learned more about this family and the terrible heartache they were trying to recover from.

One night after dining in *Little Brick*, Kim began to tell the story: "It was just an ordinary Tuesday morning in February. I was home alone in Canistota with my three kids when six-year-old J.T. came running in my room saying, 'Fire! Mommy, Mommy, fire!' I sent him outside and ran into the back bedroom and found it was full of flames. That's where Jaycob and Natasha were ..." Kim's voice began to tremble with emotion and her eyes filled with tears. "I panicked. I put Jaycob, who was just three years old, on the bed to pick up the baby. Natasha was just four months. But I started choking and I couldn't breathe. I knew I was going to die before I could get them out!"

Kim began to sob now, as tears streamed down her face. "I couldn't see, I couldn't find either one of them, the smoke was so thick. I just thought, 'I've got to get help! Someone has to help me save my babies!' The only thing I could even think to do was to jump out the window. Then I thought, 'I have to get back inside. I have to get my babies!' But a firefighter held me back and they went inside instead. However, it took them 15 minute to find Jaycob and Natasha. And by that time, it was too late. They were dead."

Following her words the room was so silent all you could hear was the sound of the dishwasher humming from the kitchen. Steve, Marie, Kim, Jesse, Diane and Roger wept, as Kim finished telling them about the tragedy that killed their beloved children and grandchildren. Kim went on to explain that a halogen lamp, which had a safety cage on it, had tipped over onto a top bunk bed, starting the bedding on fire. After a while Steve cleared his throat and spoke,

"There's nothing I can say to take away your family's pain. But I can tell you that no matter what happens to us, we always get another opportunity. God always gives us more to be grateful for, even after the worst tragedies like this one. The wonderful richness in life is that we get more chances to start again. I know that you and Jesse will be blessed with more children; please, just turn to God and don't turn away from him."

Kim and Jesse both took Steve's words to heart. They had been struggling with their faith since that fateful February day. But they knew in their hearts that Steve was right, and they renewed their determination to turn toward God in their grief.

A few years later, Kim and Jesse went on to have five more children. Kim always felt that Steve and Marie were ordained to come into their lives at that very time when they needed them the most and that it was no coincidence.

For not only did Steve and Marie help console the family following the tragic fire, Steve was also there for Roger when he ended up in the hospital after bad crash. Roger plowed into a semi-truck and was in critical condition. Diane called Steve to let him know about the accident, and Steve promised he'd make the two-hour drive to Sioux Falls in the morning.

Upon entering Roger's hospital room, Steve asked all of his relatives, except Diane, to leave. Steve felt nervous about what he was about to say; he still worried about how people would perceive him and was afraid of rejection. But he felt a strong tug at his heart about what he felt he was supposed to tell Roger. Steve cleared his throat and took hold of Roger's weathered hand:

"Roger, I can't believe you survived that horrific crash. But the fact that you have tells me it's time I share something with you."

Steve couldn't tell if Roger was receptive to what he was about to say by the blank look in his eyes, but he continued on anyway. "We've both drank a lot of beer and lived filthy lives, haven't we, Roger?"

Roger slowly nodded; that was the only cue Steve needed to go on.

"I feel obligated to tell you this because I want you to make it to Heaven, I love you that much." Steve thought of how proud Harley would be of him in this moment. This is exactly what his dad would have wanted him to do. He felt as if Harley was watching. Steve then asked Roger, "Will you pray with me?"

Roger squeezed Steve's hand in response, so Steve began his simple prayer:

"Dear God, Roger and I are here together, both of us have sinned, both fallen short, both lived a life that was filthy. Dear Jesus, come in and cleanse my heart and Roger's heart. Please

forgive us and find us worthy, so if you call us home today, we'll meet in Heaven."

Roger squeezed Steve's hand again and when he looked up, he saw tears streaming down his craggy face. He glanced over to the corner of the room where Diane was sitting and saw that she was crying as well. While Roger's and Diane's marriage had seen more than its fair share of downs, Diane credits Steve with leading Roger to the Lord.

Roger never did fully recover from that accident and a subsequent heart surgery. Two years later when he died, Steve and Marie attended his funeral in Pierre. The pastor clearly had never met Roger; it was obvious by the trite eulogy he gave. The longtime manual laborer had led a very hard life. Steve asked if he could get up and say something as well, and the pastor agreed.

"Roger, well, he wasn't always the easiest to get along with and he didn't always make the best choices in his life," Steve began. "But in the years I knew him, he strove to deepen his faith and become a better man. And while I may have thought I was helping Roger through his struggles after surgery, he also helped me. He helped strengthen my faith because I could see Christ in him."

Steve went on to tell some funny stories about Roger, the fisherman, and he left everyone at the small service smiling. Roger's family was grateful to Steve for speaking that day because his words were of great comfort to them.

Sometimes Steve and Marie simply were not able to help someone, even when that person claimed they wanted it. But that didn't mean that God couldn't still use them to touch lives.

Josh Sherman came into *Little Brick* from the neighboring town of Burke one cold January afternoon with his girlfriend, Amelia Anderson. It was an unusual day for anyone to get ice cream because temperatures had dropped below zero. But the funky chicken out front of *Little Brick* had captured their attention and its reputation for the best ice cream around had reached their ears.

Amelia looked a decade younger than her 43 years. She was in great shape and had frosted blonde hair. Amelia was known for her love of strays, often adopting new puppies and rescuing raccoons, which she kept as pets. Josh was like one of those strays that Amelia was trying to rescue. He was 10 years her junior and ruggedly masculine with a head of shaggy dark hair.

The couple slid into a corner booth. Steve introduced himself and told the couple a few jokes, making them forget their troubles for a moment. He and Josh hit it off right away. Steve suggested they order some of his famous chicken before they have ice cream, and they agreed. Steve couldn't help but notice that Amelia's cheeks were tear-stained.

"Is there anything else I can get you?" Steve asked the couple after they ordered their food.

"Help," Josh announced matter-of-factly.

While Josh expected the jovial man before him to be taken aback, Steve was not. He'd come to expect this kind of thing; not much at all surprised him anymore.

"At your service," Steve smiled. "What can I help with?" he asked gently, his voice lowering.

His compassionate tone brought Amelia, who looked as if she were about to lose it, to tears. Through her sobs she choked, "He's on meth! He can't get off of it!"

"I see," Steve nodded. Then he began to talk about his past and drinking and how he'd reached a low point in his life. Then he asked, "Can we pray together?"

The couple glanced at one another and each nodded. Steve slid into the booth next to Amelia and asked them to join hands with him:

"Lord, I know you are here with us," Steve began to pray. *"Have mercy on Josh and Amelia. Please heal Josh from his addiction and keep them close to you. Guide their every step and let them feel your love, God."*

Then Steve turned to Josh and offered, "If you're serious about getting off the drugs, I know where you can get help, real help! There's a program in Brookings with a 98 percent success rate ..." But before he had a chance to continue, Josh interrupted him,

"But that costs too much! I can't afford it!"

"It *is* expensive: eighteen thousand dollars. But if you'll commit yourself to getting better, I can help you with that," Steve offered.

"Thank you," Josh replied. "We'll talk it over."

Steve got up and left the couple to converse, and a short while later brought them their chicken dinners. When he returned with their ice cream, he offered a few more words of encouragement and blessings. Their spirits seemed brighter as they left. Steve was hopeful that Josh would take him up on his offer. But Steve never knew what to expect in these situations.

Steve took Josh's story, without revealing his name, to the various churches in Platte. He asked for sponsors to support Josh through treatment and for donations to help pay for it. Once he had it all lined up, he called Josh who promised to show up at *Little Brick* the following Tuesday at 10 a.m. Amelia had asked Josh to move out because he continued to use meth and because he knew he was going to lose her, Josh now seemed more motivated to get treatment.

One the day he was supposed to arrive, Steve waited patiently in *Little Brick* as 10 turned into 11 and then into noon. He called Amelia to ask her if Josh was coming. Josh had promised her that he would go get treatment and meet up with Steve that day. Amelia told Steve she would get ahold of Josh and get back to him.

When Josh answered Amelia's call, she said, "Steve has raised all the money put a team together for you. He's done all this for you! He believes in you and thinks you have potential. Are you just going to throw it all away? Are you not even going to try?"

"I don't think the problem is the drugs," Josh said, deep in denial. "I think I'm just addicted to you. I can get off the drugs on my own."

"You're so wrong, Josh. Why can't you see that?" Amelia began to sob. She told Josh he could call her again, but only when he was clean. Then she called Steve back to give him the news.

"I'm so sorry, Amelia. If Josh continues down this path, he's going to be staring death straight in the face. But remember that Marie and I love you and you are a woman of God. Sometimes the hardest lesson to learn is when it is time to walk away. But we are here for you. Don't ever forget that. And we will continue to pray for Josh."

It was a reminder that Amelia desperately needed. A few weeks later Amelia stopped in to *Little Brick* on her way through town.

"Well hello there, young lady! Great to see you!" Steve welcomed Amelia with a big grin "How's it going?"

A wave of emotion passed over Amelia's face as she answered,

"It's okay ... now." She said, followed by a pause. There was so much more than words could express in the silence of that moment. "You see, Josh went back to smoking meth. I begged and pleaded with him to take you up on your offer. But the drug has such a powerful hold on him. I was devastated. But I remembered when we prayed together, how a sense of peace overcame me. I felt hopeful for the first time in a long time. I stopped arguing with Josh about what he was doing and I told him that I would be there for him, if he got help, but that I couldn't be his girlfriend anymore while he was using. And then I went to church. I hadn't been to church in quite a while. I'd drifted away from my faith. But it was amazing. I didn't feel alone anymore. I'm sad about Josh choosing the drugs over me. But I kept going to church and I felt better and better. I have hope once again. I just wanted to come in here and thank you."

As she told her story, tears of joy began to run down Steve's face. *The Lord does work in mysterious ways!* He thought he was called to help Josh that day and he felt deeply sadden by Josh's decision, but at the same time he was ecstatic that his encounter with the couple had bought Amelia back to Christ. *God knows what he's doing*, Steve thought.

He embraced Amelia, giving her a big bear hug and telling her how happy it made him to hear that she was now a believer and that he had helped make that happen. Then the two them joined hands to pray for Josh. From that day onward, Amelia and Steve have remained close friends. And Steve has helped Amelia remain strong in her resolve to not take Josh back until he goes through drug treatment. His offer to Josh for help stands as long as necessary.

* * *

Most of the people God called on Steve to reach walked through the doors of *Little Brick* by their own accord, but some of them Steve brought in himself, such as a trucker passing through town. One evening, he was walking out of the Platte Food Center, when a man driving a semi pulled up next to him in the parking lot and rolled down his window.

"Hey, buddy," the man called out. He was big, about 6 foot, 2 inches and 250 pounds. He had jet-black hair and a salt-and-pepper beard. "I was wondering where I could go around here to gamble?"

"You're taking a gamble just driving around the streets of Platte!" Steve joked. But then he went on to tell the stranger that there wasn't much for gambling in Platte. Steve added that the closest casino was Fort Randall in Lake Andes, on the Yankton Sioux Indian Reservation, which was about 40 miles away.

"But if you really want to gamble, come down to my restaurant, *Little Brick* and try out my broasted chicken!"

"Sounds good!" the trucker said, agreeably.

Moments later the two men were in *Little Brick* and Steve was putting the chicken in the fryer. As the chicken browned in the grease, he said to the trucker:

"I'm Steve Frey. It's a pleasure to meet you!"

"I'm Paul Miller," the man said in a gruff voice.

Steve looked into his eyes, trying to assess just how open this man might be to the message Steve felt compelled to pass on to all who entered through his doors.

"I'll tell you what," Steve said, "The chicken is on me, if I can sit down with you and share my story."

Paul raised an eyebrow, but wasn't about to pass up a free meal.

"Suit yourself," he said.

"Great!" Steve proclaimed, and he rushed back into the kitchen to retrieve the cooked chicken. He piled the chicken high on the plate and then tossed some of the potato wedges, which were under the warmer, on the side.

He walked back out into the restaurant with the plate and placed it in front of Paul. The smell of grease and chicken filled Paul's nostrils and his stomach growled. Steve slid into the seat opposite of Paul and stayed silent for a moment, while Paul picked up a piece of the meat with his hands and took a large bite.

"Mmmmm! This is good!" Paul licked his lips and he finished his initial taste. As he went into for the second bite, Steve began his testimony.

"I bet you're on the road a lot. See a lot of places and a lot of things, huh?"

"I sure do," Paul replied, dabbing the grease off his mouth with a napkin. I drive close to three thousand miles a week!"

"Wow, that is a lot," Steve affirmed. "I spent a lot of time on the road myself for a few years, not driving truck or anything, but just sort of drifting. It got pretty lonely."

Paul nodded and looked down at his plate of chicken and potatoes.

"Yeah, *that it does,*" he agreed.

"See, the thing is, I used to gamble and drink and chase a lot of women. I was looking for something to take away the dull ache of loneliness and misery. But all the gambling, all the booze and all the women — none of it did. In fact, I felt even more empty."

There was a long pause, so Steve continued: "I didn't fill up that emptiness inside of me until I turned my life over to Jesus Christ and let him fill it." Steve paused and noticed that Paul had put his chicken down and was looking at his plate again.

"Am I offending you?" Steve asked.

"No," Paul offered in a small voice for such a large man.

And that was the only opening Steve needed to continue his story. As he spoke about the low points in his life and how, once he prayed and offered himself up to Christ, he was able to go on and see the beauty in life and still love others, he noticed that the big burly trucker had begun to cry.

"It's okay," Steve told him. "Whatever it is, it's okay. Christ loves you and I love you," Steve professed.

"It's my marriage!" Paul spurted out as he wiped a tear out of the corner of his eye. Paul went on to tell Steve about how all his hours on the road and his gambling had taken their toll on his marriage. His wife had just told him over the phone this morning that she was leaving him.

"I love my wife. But it's probably too late," Paul said with regret.

"I don't believe it is!" Steve assured him. "God put me in that parking lot at just the right moment, Paul! Can we pray together?"

Paul agreed and the two men bowed their heads and Steve began to pray:

"Dear Father, please help this man Paul, named after the founder of the Christian Church; your own disciple. Please heal his heart and his wife's heart and restore their marriage. Thank you, God, for bringing Paul into my sight today, so that You could help Paul have a better future through You. Please bless Paul and his wife, amen."

As Steve finished the prayer, Paul echoed his "amen" and it looked as if a weight had been lifted off his strong shoulders. A short time later, after Paul had finished his meal and stood up to leave, the two men shook hands, and then Steve brought him in for a hug. As he pounded the large man's back, he said, "Now stay in touch! Let me know how it goes and feel free to stop in here anytime! Your next meal is on the house, too!"

Paul had given Steve his number and a couple of weeks

later Steve got a text:

Thanks for the chicken and prayer. We're trying to work it out. Please keep praying for us!

Steve closed his flip phone and said a silent prayer, thanking God for bringing all these people into his life.

Steve also began to get invitations from area churches to speak to various congregations and tell his story of hope. Even schools invited him in to share his message. He spoke at Sunshine Bible Academy for their Thanksgiving banquet and surprised his audience by playing Elvis Presley's song, *The Wonder of You*. The line, *"I'll guess I'll never know the reason why you love me like you do; that's the wonder, the wonder of you,"* seemed to sum up God's love for Steve.

It seemed an odd thing to hear the king of rock 'n' roll being played during a Christian sermon. But Steve turned his back to the crowd as Elvis's rich voice filled the auditorium, and the lyrics moved him to tears. Elvis might have been singing about a female lover, but to Steve his words were a tribute to the greatest lover of all — God.

After that, Steve was invited to speak to Wessington Springs High School students and to Dakota Christian School. He brought his message to Rotary Clubs and to the McCrossan Boys' Ranch in Sioux Falls, whose mission was to help troubled boys get on the right track.

Autumn is arguably the best season in South Dakota. Days are still warm, with an edge of crispness and the sun is usually shining. It can always be windy on the prairie, but in the fall, there are more calm days than not. It was on one such Chamber of Commerce day when a couple in their early 60s walked through the doors of *Little Brick*. Dwight and Nancy Miller were looking for dinner, after discovering that the Pizza Ranch in Platte was closed. The Millers, who lived in the Omaha suburb of Bellevue, often stopped in Platte on their way to or from the Black Hills. They enjoyed staying at a bed and breakfast in town called Molly's Manor, a renovated 1918 home that was originally owned by Swedish immigrants.

But this was their first time in Steve's and Marie's shop. Immediately upon entering, Steve approached the couple and made a few recommendations off the menu, including his now locally famous fried chicken. Dwight and Nancy were charmed by Steve's jovial personality and when Steve asked them if they minded if he sat down with them after their food arrived, they gladly agreed. It wasn't long before Steve began telling them some of the stories of his life. And Steve never told a story without giving all the glory to God.

"Do you love Jesus?" Steve asked.

The couple nodded, "yes" they did, and Dwight, who was a deacon in his Baptist church at home, welcomed Steve's testimony. Then suddenly Dwight felt moved to say, "What are you doing on October 14th?"

"I think I'm going to be speaking at a church in Bellevue!" Steve stated matter-of-factly.

"It's our pastor appreciation day, and I'd really appreciate it if you'd come!" Dwight said with a big smile on his face.

Steve agreed, and before they left he shared his story about the three largest fish he'd ever caught and the message he received from God during that unbelievable experience. Dwight, a fisherman himself, was quite impressed by his fish tale. Within a week of returning home, Dwight grabbed his rod and reel and headed for a lake in eastern Nebraska. Moments after casting his line, Dwight pulled in the biggest largemouth bass he'd ever caught and he'd been fishing in the area since the 1960s. But that wasn't the end of Dwight's Big Fish Story. A few weeks later, he visited another lake in the area for an afternoon of fishing, and moments after his bait hit the water, another gigantic largemouth bass was on his line. Dwight couldn't believe it; the very same thing that had happened to Steve was also happening to him. He did a little dance of joy right then with his catch in hand.

Within days, he was back on the water, but this time at a different lake and he'd brought along his son and grandson. Once again, within moments of casting out his line he felt a tug. This time he reeled in an even more gigantic largemouth bass, about five pounds. Dwight realized how remarkable it was to catch such three large fish in one season in eastern Nebraska. That night he called Steve and told him that he now had his own Big Fish Story.

"Sometimes that's just the way the Lord talks to you," Steve said with certainty.

The following month, Steve made the trip to Bellevue to speak at the Lighthouse Baptist Church where Dwight served as deacon. Dwight got up and introduced him to the congregation and explained that he had met Steve at his ice cream shop and restaurant *Little Brick* in Platte.

"The love starts when you enter the door and doesn't stop when you leave," Dwight told his parishioners about his encounter with Steve at *Little Brick.*

Word spread about Steve's speaking engagements and soon other churches in the region called to ask him to make an appearance. And Steve never turned them down. Suddenly he really *was* following in Harley's footsteps, so many years after members in his West Union congregation recognized the potential in him. And just like when they were traveling around selling pies in grocery stores, Marie always accompanied him. She took her place in the audience for his sermons and when their eyes locked, Steve saw the love and encouragement on her face. He would also see members of his audiences wiping away tears of their own as he shared his pain and his salvation.

Chapter 22: *Beauty for Ashes*

"To appoint unto them that mourn in Zion, to give unto them beauty for ashes, the oil of joy for mourning, the garment of praise for the spirit of heaviness, that they might be called trees of righteousness, the planting of the LORD, *that He might be glorified."* Isaiah 61:3

No one could have imagined or have been prepared for the unthinkable, really the unspeakable, tragedy that rocked Platte on Sept. 17, 2015. Neither Steve nor any of the high school kids who filled up *Little Brick* that day could have predicted it. In the early morning hours, Scott Westerhuis used a gun, given to him by a friend, to murder his four children and his wife. He then set his home on fire and killed himself. Scott's world had come crashing down on him when he was about to finally be exposed for embezzling millions of dollars in federal grant money. Scott made the fateful decision that he would not go out alone; he would take his entire family with him.

The fallout from the horrific act was now statewide news, as more evidence of Scott's wrongdoing became public. South Dakota's Attorney General even held two news conferences in Platte's Community Center. In one he announced the findings of the death investigation. Attorney General Marty Jackley told people in the small town that Scott Westerhuis had acted alone in carrying out the murders of his family and burning down their home. In a later news conference, Mr. Jackley announced that he was filing charges against three other people who worked closely with Scott and his wife Nicole. They were accused of taking part in the conspiracy to hide the misuse of grant funds.

All of the difficult times in Steve's life, up until now, had groomed him for this moment. It was *now* that the young people in town — many of whom he considered close friends — would need him the most.

The Platte-Geddes sophomore class piled into *Little Brick* the following day, and Steve greeted the grieving high school students with hugs and a compassionate heart. The idea of a father killing his children was incomprehensible to these teenagers. If that could happen to Michael Westerhuis, a boy whom they'd known since kindergarten, what in the world could happen to them? Many questioned Steve, "How could God let this happen?"

Steve invited the kids to pray with him in the back of the shop. As Steve began to pray for the souls of the Westerhuis children and the broken hearts of the teens before him, tears filled 15-year-old Chase Pheifer's eyes as he thought about his good friend, Michael, leaving *Little Brick* just the day before and offering another classmate a ride. Chase was among the closest to Steve out of all the teens. He'd met Steve when he was just nine-years-old, when Steve ran the farmers' market in town. Since then, the two had developed a close friendship, and Steve hired Chase to mow his lawn and invited Chase and his friends to use his hot tub and fire pit in his backyard anytime they'd like.

"I don't understand how a loving God could allow a man to kill his entire family!" Chase angrily choked out the words.

"I don't either," Steve said, empathetically. "But I do believe you're looking at it all wrong. God didn't *allow* Scott to kill his wife and children. God gave us all free will. I'm not going to pretend to have the answers about why these evil things happen. But I am going to tell you that God's love will prevail. Michael and his brother and sisters all had faith. They are now in Heaven with Jesus Christ. They suffer from pain and sorrow no more!" Steve proclaimed.

Chase began to cry, and some of the other students gathered around him.

"Horrible things will happen," Steve continued. "But God does not leave you alone, without any help, to deal with them. I can guarantee you that! This is the time for you to all lean on each other and look to one another for love and support. I love you all. I am here for you anytime you need to talk or just need someone to tell you that they love you!"

The kids began to hug one another. They gradually left in small groups and went home to their families. Steve locked up the shop after they were all gone and dropped to his knees right in from of the ice cream case. *"God, you have gotten me through the worst times in my life. Thank You for giving me new life through You! Please show me how I can help these poor suffering children. I will do anything You want me to! Please show me the way!"* he prayed.

Steve went home that night feeling troubled. He tossed and turned, barely sleeping a wink, as he thought about the poor Westerhuis children and their final moments on earth. He also couldn't stop thinking about the sorrow in the eyes of the high school students who had shown up at *Little Brick.* He wanted so badly to end their pain, but he just didn't know how to do that. He waited for some sign from God.

Meanwhile, the memorial services were held for Nicole Westerhuis and the four Westerhuis children. Scott Westerhuis' funeral was held separately in a different church, and he was buried in a family cemetery apart from his wife and children. Nearly a month passed and Steve still had no idea how he could help the grieving teens. It seemed that with each day that passed, the grim reality of the family's deaths became more real and difficult to take. Every day there were news stories on the investigation into what happened during those early morning hours of the murders and suicide. Nobody in town felt they could escape the crushing weight of the shame and notoriety that one of their own had carried out such a despicable act.

An idea began to take shape in the back of Steve's mind as the days went on. After closing *Little Brick* one evening when some of the teens still felt down and depressed, he announced to Marie, "I know I need to do something, Marie! And now I think I know what it is! I'm going to get each of the players on the football team a dog tag and have it engraved with Michael's number — 28. And then I need to tell them my story."

Marie nodded, "I think that's a great idea, Steve. Let's invite them over for lunch in a couple of weeks and you can do that."

"You're the best, Marie!" Steve said, grinning.

He was a little nervous. He knew that the loss of a friend could make teenagers consider taking their own lives. And he felt it was time to tell them all that he had been there. He knew what it felt like to be so depressed that he wanted to end it all. He believed that if he told them about how he had nearly killed himself, but was saved by the grace of God, his story would give them hope.

Steve and Marie ordered sterling silver dog tags with a small diamond on them. Steve didn't care about the cost. He wanted them to be special and something the students could keep and even wear forever. On each one he had engraved, *#28 Strong*. After the medals arrived, he invited the members of the Platte-Geddes football team and Michael's girlfriend Lizzy to join him for lunch at *Little Brick.*

At noon on Dec. 11, 2015, the team members filled *Little Brick* over their lunch hour. Some of their parents had joined them as well. Steve looked over the crowd; he was excited to present each boy and Lizzy with their mementos to the friend they had lost. He looked at 17-year-old Jason Hofer. *That poor kid!* he mused. Jason has lost both his parents in unrelated illnesses in the last year. *How could he handle another loss?* The kids loaded up on chicken, potatoes and nachos — the kind with that bright yellow, processed cheese sauce — and made their way back to their seats. Then Steve called out in a loud voice:

"I've asked you all to come here today, because I have something for you and I want to share something about myself with you. You see, there's a part of my life you don't know about. I made a bad decision years ago. I had enlisted in the Vietnam War and when I returned back to the U.S., I was involved in a farm accident where a little girl died. I wasn't in my right mind and I left my wife and three children. And I only took 50 dollars and put it in my pocket. I lost my farm and my home and my family and everything. I ran away. I was living a pathetic lifestyle because I became very bitter. I was very, very bitter. I was mad at the world."

Steve wanted the students to really hear the depths of his despair in order for them to know that he was able to understand theirs. He continued, "But you're my best friends and I want you to know this! I was going to take my own life, and I couldn't do it. Instead, I knelt down and I said, 'Jesus, if you're there, I need help.' I asked forgiveness for everything I'd done; the people I'd hurt."

Steve looked at the young faces, wracked in pain and guilt over the loss of their friend and went on to tell them that ever since he turned his life over to Christ it had been filled with peace and purpose.

"I'm not promising you a perfect life, but if you'll make God a part of it, He will help you get through anything! We've gone through a very tough time together. You people are champions. You've carried yourself like men and women. I want to give you something that you can keep for the next twenty years so you can remember how strong you really are," Steve told them.

And with those words, he presented each student with a dog tag in remembrance of Michael. As he put one around each student's neck, he offered him or her a small blessing,

"Chase, you're important to me, man!" Steve said as he placed the medal over Chase's head.

"Onward 28 strong; in memory of Michael, I want you to wear this with pride."

"Thank you," Chase replied.

Then he turned to Jason: "Jason, you're important to me, man!"

"Thank you, Frey!" Jason said.

And so it went, one by one, as Steve professed his love for each boy in a way they could appreciate and understand.

He presented Lizzy with the final dog tag saying, "You keep that forever, Lizzy!"

"Okay, thank you," Lizzy muttered through her tears.

Then he turned and faced the students and their parents, fully realizing that all the ups and downs in his life had led him to this moment in which he could be there for these children.

""I know that you have to keep going forward. There are many times I wanted to end it, but now I'm glad I didn't because now I can help you. And I truly hope in some small way today that I have."

And anyone could tell by the lightened look on their faces that *he had helped them*. Steve embraced each teen as they left his restaurant, letting them know he was there for them if they ever wanted to talk. And from that day on he would be transformed in their eyes, from the quirky, jolly, old codger, who enjoyed their company and gave them a heck of a deal on chicken into a true lifelong friend.

Steve became a spiritual guidepost for many of them, such as Chase and Jason, who spent hours in his company. It was in the deepening of their understanding of the world, grounded in faith, which proved to be Steve's true reward. And while Steve and Marie would never get rich on all-you-can-eat chicken buffets for $5, they felt truly wealthy with the blessings bestowed by God in the form of each person who walked through the doors of *Little Brick*. For there was no doubt in Steve's mind that he had been ordained by God to let each and every one of them know *THEY WERE LOVED*.

To view the KELOLAND News story on Steve Frey with the Platte High School students, click here:
http://www.keloland.com/news/article/featured-stories/-28-strong

Epilogue: A Word from Steve Frey

"But you will receive power when the Holy Spirit has come upon you, and you will be my witnesses in Jerusalem and in all Judea and Samaria, and to the end of the earth." Acts 1:8

After all of my ups and downs in life, I now realize my mission, my true purpose. Jesus followed me through my days, even the darkest ones, protecting me and calling me to come to him. Jesus asked me to submit myself *entirely* to him, seven days a week, 24 hours a day, through good times and bad. When I finally yielded to Jesus' will, He blessed me tremendously.

Jesus forgave me, rebuilt my life and gave me my very own mission to accomplish for Him. That mission is to lead all others whom I meet to Jesus Christ. His salvation is always here for us. All we have to do is ask Jesus to forgive us and He will do all the rest. Never, ever give up on Christ. Many, many times throughout our lives, we must ask for forgiveness in order to start over. But Jesus said, *'I will never leave you, nor forsake you." Hebrews 13:5.* He also said, *"Come unto me all ye that labor and are heavy laden and I will give you rest." Matthew 11:28.*

It took me years to realize what my dad, Harley, was trying to teach me. But this Bible verse sums it up much better than I ever could myself: *"I beseech you therefore, brethren, by the mercies of God, that ye present your bodies a living sacrifice, holy, acceptable unto God, which is your reasonable service. And be not conformed to this world: but be ye transformed by the renewing of your mind, that ye may prove what is that good, and acceptable, and perfect, will of God." Romans 12:1-2*

I would also like to leave you, dear reader, with this verse to ponder for your own salvation: *"Let not your heart be troubled; ye believe in God, believe also in me. In my Father's house are many mansions: if it were not so, I would have told you. I go prepare a place for you. I will come again and receive you unto myself; that where I am, there ye may be also. And whither I go ye know and the way ye know. Thomas saith unto him, Lord, we know not whither thou goest: and how can we know the way? Jesus saith unto him, I am the way, the truth and the life: no man cometh into the Father, but by me."* John 14:1-6.

Jesus is coming soon and he has a place for me, right beside my earthly father. As you read my personal story, I pray that each one of you will come to know Jesus Christ, the King of Kings and Lord of Lords; and that on a very personal level he may reign in your life daily!

God Bless You,
Steve Frey

Photo: Chad Phillips

Made in the USA
Lexington, KY
23 April 2018